Swimhiking   ...ain and
Europe

Peter Hayes

Published by
Gilbert Knowle Publishers
6 Valeside
Durham DH1 4RF
England

© Peter Hayes 2022

ISBN: 978-1-9998871-4-8 (hardback)

ISBN: 978-1-9998871-5-5 (paperback)

In memory of Mary Hayes (1943-2020)

Preface

This book describes and maps swimhikes in Britain and fifteen other European countries: Holland, France, Italy, Croatia, Bosnia, Greece, Turkey, Cyprus, Spain, Switzerland, Austria, Germany, Hungary, Portugal (Madeira) and Monaco.

To swimhike through a place engages your body to the full. It is immersive; it gives an intense feeling of being alive to the moment. But another kind of deeper experience also awaits if you can touch the past of the area you are exploring. So, wherever a swimhike may be, I have tried to add something, often a story, that I hope gives at least a glimpse of the history of the place and of the people who have lived there. Some of these stories are open to doubt. However, I have aimed to be as truthful as possible, and in the great majority of cases I honestly believe that what I have written is probably true. Only very occasionally do I think that it probably isn't.

Contents

Introduction

Swimhiking
Swimhiking combines swimming with walking or running in a continuous journey in which you enter the water in one place, get out at another, and carry on. Swimming, therefore, forms a part of your hike. It is not a question of walking to water, say a river, and then leaving your clothes on the bank to have a swim before coming out at the same place. When equipped to go swimhiking, you are not tied to your entry point like this, as you can swim across the river and keep going on the other side, or float downstream before returning to land and hiking on. You can do this because you are carrying your clothes and whatever else you need, such as food and drink, with you in some kind of swimsac.

A swimsac
In a pamphlet (*Swimsac: a rucksack for swimming and hiking*, Beamish: 2005) and in *Swimhiking in The Lake District and North East England* (Durham: Gilbert Knowle, 2008, 2018) I described how to make a swimsac. Almost nobody did. My friends and relatives simply expected me to lend them one of mine, or preferably give it to them. Other people loved the idea of swimhiking but when it came to making a bag, a typical conversation would go something like this:

Other Person: Hey, swimhiking! That's a *great* idea! Where can I buy a swimsac?
Peter: You can't. You have to make one yourself.
Other Person: What? Eh? Ugh?

A spasm of helplessness passes over them. I might as well have said make your own moon rocket. We live in an age of advanced manufacturing and mass consumerism, and in that age, you just do not make things yourself.

Now that swimhiking has started taking off, lots of swimsacs of various designs, usually involving some kind of towing system, have

8

become available. However, it is still perfectly easy to make one, and this is how.

How to Make a Swimsac
These are the things you need:

*rucksack with:
   (a) drawstring (not a zip)
   (b) chest/sternum strap
   (c) waist strap
   (d) side pockets
*roll-top drybag
(Ortlieb bags work well)
*double-chambered child's armband
*cheap plastic shopping bag
*pair of scissors

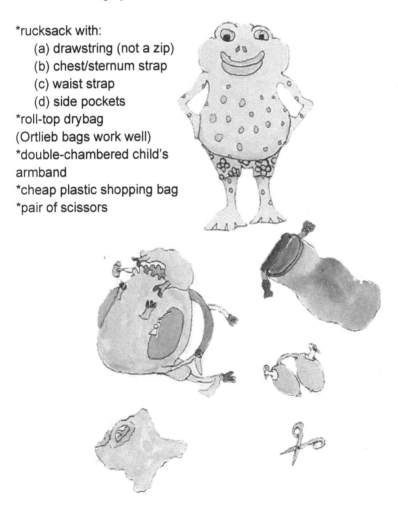

To create your swimsac:

1. Cut holes in the back of the rucksack, and in the shoulder and waist straps, to rip out any soft padding—which absorbs water. (Hard padding can stay in.)

2. Cut the armband in half and put one chamber in each side pocket.

3. Put the plastic bag (which is for your shoes) into the drybag, and the drybag into the rucksack.

Voila! You now have a swimsac.

How to use a swimsac
On land, use your swimsac just as you would a rucksack. When you reach the water:

1. Change into your swimsuit.

2. Put your shoes into the plastic bag and put that bag, your clothes, towel (a thin towel is best to save space), and anything else you want to keep dry into the drybag.

3. Roll up and seal the drybag, put it in the outer sac (the rucksack) and close the hood.

4. If you have not already done so, blow up the armbands in the side pockets.

5. Do not put straps over your shoulders. Instead, clip the chest strap UNDER your shoulders, and the waist strap around your waist. Straps should be moderately firm but not tight.

You are now ready to start swimming. You will find that the bag will not weigh you down at all. When you get out, change back into your dry clothes and start walking or running again.

You do not *always* need a swimsac to go swimhiking. Some tough swimhikers merely stuff one or two things in their wetsuit, which they wear both in the water and on the land. For short swimhikes on a warm day all you might need are beach shoes or, if the soles of your feet are hard enough, you can wear nothing but a swimming suit, or indeed nothing.

Why go swimhiking?
Since the invention of boats and bridges, swimhiking has been an almost entirely useless activity, but it is fun. Somewhere in our past we must have been amphibious-like creatures and swimhiking allows us to realise this side to our nature. A swimhiking journey can be challenging or gentle, but it is always engaging and imaginative. Swimhiking expands the boundaries of what we can do in the countryside—or indeed the town—and lets us explore and experience up-close the mixture of land and water that forms our world. Swimhiking involves no mechanical aids and has minimal equipment, making it both inexpensive and environmentally friendly. It is accessible to almost everyone and can be enjoyed as much by families as by athletes. Indeed, in my experience, swimhiking is ideal in every respect apart from one: when swimhiking on holiday, I have never quite worked out what to do with a damp swimsac after returning to the hotel, especially if we don't have a balcony.

What the book covers
Europe offers infinite possibilities to the swimhiker and this has made it difficult to know when to stop swimhiking and start writing. At first, I imagined putting it off until I was sat in an old people's home peering at my maps and reliving old memories. But even at the age of 58, this still seems quite a long way off. What if I never get there? And if I *am* lucky enough to reach a ripe old age, it may well be that by that time I won't feel like writing a book, preferring to spend my final hours on earth enjoying daytime TV. Then I considered putting things off until I had completed at least one swimhike in every country of Europe. "But," I thought to myself, "do I *really* want to troop off to inconvenient places like Belarus and Moldova etc, when I could be enjoying yet another package holiday on the Mediterranean? No." So I have written the book now. As a result, it is rather patchy. There is nothing about Belarus or Moldova. Nothing either about Serbia, Montenegro, Albania,

12

Macedonia, Slovenia, San Marino, Malta, Bulgaria, Romania, Poland, The Czech Republic, Slovakia, any of the Scandinavian or Baltic states, Ireland, Finland, Iceland, Belgium, Luxembourg, Liechtenstein, Russia, Andorra, or Ukraine. Sorry about that.

What happens in the book?
There is another problem with my book. Nothing very much happens in it. If, for example, you are reading about a climb up Mount Everest or somewhere similar, you can confidently expect that a few mountaineers and their loyal Sherpas will die under tragic circumstances, and that even if they don't, someone will plunge into a crevasse and break both legs and be left for dead, until they squeeze out from a hole in a glacier three weeks later having survived in the interim on lichen and salamanders. But my swimhikes pass by remarkably smoothly. Aided by my swimsac I bob around like a cork in the water, unsinkable. Nothing tries to eat me. With caution, not to say cowardice, I keep well away from danger, and only once or twice has it really managed to get very far creeping up on me unawares. On one occasion I am almost carried off by a current (Church Rock), on another I am stung by lots of jellyfish (Menorca). The most dangerous occasion of all occurred after I cut my big toe on a strand of pebbles swimhiking in my local river, the Wear. When, some days later, the toe swells up, I fail to draw the connection and go to the doctor with a misdiagnosis based on an afternoon's research on the internet: I have decided that I have gout, brought on by excessive drinking during my most recent package holiday on the Med. (This was in Turkey, which as it is at least partly in Europe, I have included in the guide.) The GP examines my foot and peers knowingly at my red nose. He agrees with me: yes, it is almost certainly gout, and prescribes some pills. And all the while, visible beneath my skin, a roseate line of blood poisoning is slowly snaking its way up my leg. Were this a proper adventure story, this is where I would meet my end, or at least have to amputate my own limb using whatever tools were at hand. But it is not, and once the infection is recognised for what it is, I am simply put on penicillin.

Safety in numbers?
I do not wish to create the impression that swimhiking is completely safe because there is an obvious risk of drowning. Beaches, rivers and lakes are the scenes of tragic accidents, and when you go

swimhiking, you are inevitably taking some chance, even if only a tiny one, of coming to grief. The routes I describe are designed to be *nice* rather than *hard*, so there is no particular reason for you to drown on them, but still, you never know.

There are various well-meaning bits of advice about how to minimise the drowning risk (for sea swimming I give my own advice in the discussion of Church Rock). However, I am not sure how helpful they are. In particular, I doubt the frequent suggestion that you are safer if you have someone with you. It is true that if *you* start to drown, whoever you are with can do their best to rescue you. But what if *they* start to drown, and when you try and help, they pull you down as well? Also, when you head off entirely on your own, you have an instinctive realisation that the water you are stepping into is a part of nature: awesome, enormous, beautiful and pitiless. In other words, you have a sense of your own mortality, and so act with a due sense of caution. When you are in a group, such feelings tend to vanish; it is all a bit of lark, and you egg each other on.

Signs that cry wolf
Signs—particularly common in England—may tell you not to swim (including on some of the routes in this book). Sometimes, signs are simply officious and can be ignored. However, on other occasions they may warn of a genuine danger that you ignore at your peril. As to which kind of sign is which, you will have to work this out for yourself.

The origins of swimhiking
I like to preen myself that I invented swimhiking, but really I only came up with the term; the idea in one form or another must been around since prehistory. In the historical record, swimhiking seems to have been mainly the preserve of soldiers and assassins: Assyrians, Samurai, various James Bond types. However, in its more peaceful form as a leisure activity, the person with the best claim to have invented swimhiking might be the Irish-American Paul Boyton (1848-1924). This pioneer had a rubber drysuit with air pockets inside to wear on his trips. The land-hiking elements of his routes were incidental and nor did he seem to swim exactly, more lie on his back and use a paddle, while pausing now and then to smoke a cigar, but there is no need to quibble about these things

too much. Boyton wrote a book about his exploits called *The Story of Paul Boyton*, one that is full of excitement. Before he has even acquired his rubber suit, Able Seaman Boyton has undertaken an improvised swimhike by deserting his ship and swimming ashore at Malaga, pushing his possessions on a plank. Once he has his rubber suit, there is no stopping him. He jumps off a transatlantic liner as it nears the coast of Ireland in a storm, and somehow survives the waves crashing against the cliffs to land safely. The fame of this exploit allows Boyton—by now mysteriously promoted to the rank of captain—to earn enough money to travel Europe, traversing its great rivers in a manner that makes the routes described here seem puny. In this book, river swimhikes are at most a few hundred yards long but Boyton floats down rivers for hundreds of miles. And wherever he goes he is menaced by death. Sometimes he is shot at, sometimes he falls down a waterfall. Even on a short swim in the Mediterranean he manages to get attacked by a shark (which he deftly slices open), whereas I—who have swum in the Med countless times—have never even *seen* one there. Also, whenever he arrives somewhere, Boyton is invariably feted by eager crowds and is quite often romanced by beautiful women. That doesn't happen to me either.

Choice of routes and locations
Occasionally I have visited a place specifically to go swimhiking. Mostly, however, I have looked around for routes on family holidays. These holiday destinations have been dictated almost entirely by finding somewhere to go that is cheap. Often this bargain holiday turns out to be by the sea, but sometimes it is not. Anyway, wherever we are at, I wake up early and go exploring with my swimsac, before getting back with a good appetite for breakfast. Now and again, I have been to a conference and done the same thing. This helps to explain why the routes are generally quite short and are sometimes at places which are not obvious locales for swimhiking. But with a bit of ingenuity, I think you can swimhike pretty much anywhere, and hope that this book will serve as an inspiration to do just that.

Ease and difficulty of swimhikes
The routes *over land* on the urban and low level swimhikes are easy. On mountain routes, the climbing involved and the ground underfoot naturally make them somewhat more difficult. The

swimhikes in Stavelely; in Scotland, and in the Rhinogs in Wales also require off-path navigation over tricky terrain (or at least a gadget that will do the navigation for you). The distances *in the water* on almost all routes are within the capabilities of a moderate swimmer on warm, calm and still days. (An exception is the Six Lochs of Glen Trool swimhike, which has a cumulative effect.) However, weather conditions can make an enormous difference to levels of difficulty: a mixture of cold, wind, rainfall and poor visibility can quickly turn an easy route into one that is wholly impossible. A few of the swimhikes include large rivers. It is easy enough to get *into* these rivers, and once you are in, it is easy to go with the flow— indeed it is impossible to do otherwise. However, as I discovered in the Ria de Bilbao, whether such rivers can be said to 'easy' to swimhike in, really depends entirely on one thing: how easy it is to get out again.

Route Maps
When preparing the maps (in no particular order) I deliberately attempted to stick to one style. Nonetheless, they gradually changed—there must have been some unconscious evolutionary process at work—so that when I got to the last map, it looked a bit different from the first. "Should I do them all again?" I wondered. No: because if I did, then they would just evolve some *more,* and I would be no further forward.

Routes are marked in red. Arrows indicate if routes are:

⊍ clockwise, or ⊍ anticlockwise.

A cross ✕ shows the start and finish point.

Although the maps give a rough idea of the routes, don't rely on them too much. In fact, don't rely too much on anything.

Part One

BRITAIN

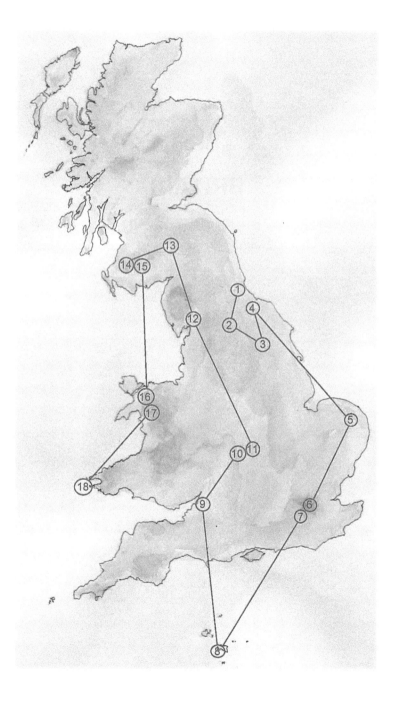

1. Durham

2. Bainbridge

3. York

4. Egglescliffe

5. Norwich

6. London

7. Chertsey

8. Portelet Bay

9. Bristol

10. Warwick

11. Leamington Spa

12. Staveley

13. Loch Skeen

14. Glen Trool

15. Loch Dee

16. Snowdonia

17. The Rhinogs

18. Pembrokeshire

England

In the early nineteenth century, England's beautiful countryside was immortalised by John Constable and other landscape painters. Although the country has now become considerably more crowded and is covered in wind triffids (to help save the planet) cars (to help destroy it) and three spike metal fences (to keep us out of it), there is still a fair amount of countryside left to explore. Meanwhile, what with sewage systems etc. the towns are surely much better than they were back then.

1. Durham

I may as well begin where I live. There are lots of places to swimhike in the Wear around Durham, particularly in the area that falls roughly between Framwellgate Bridge in the town and a pedestrian bridge with wooden slats known as 'Noisy Bridge' about two miles upriver. However, a short route beneath Prebends Bridge is my favourite. If you are lucky, otters can be seen here, eating fish, playing, blowing lines of bubbles. Once a deer jumped into the water with a great splash and, head held high, swam across the river and up the far bank. Near Noisy Bridge I see another smaller animal swimming across. What is that? A mink? No, it is a squirrel, its tail floating behind it.

A quote from Walter Scott inscribed on Prebends Bridge perfectly captures the view of the great cathedral that stands so high above, and the atmosphere it creates:

> *Grey towers of Durham*
> *Yet well I love thy mix'd and massive piles*
> *Half church of God, half castle 'gainst the Scot*
> *And long to roam these venerable aisles*
> *With records stored of deeds long since forgot*

And at Noisy Bridge the man-made part of the view is encapsulated in the words of another great poet, John Betjeman:

> *All fields we'll turn to sports grounds, lit at night*
> *From concrete standards by fluorescent light**

---

* Actually, these lines are not written on the bridge, but they should be.

22

View from Noisy Bridge

When I painted this picture, I could not bear to add in all of the lighting, fencing, advertisements, carparks, etc that now spread like a cancer from the sports complex to cover what were once open meadows on one side of the river. So I left them out.

The man on the horse
Like most people in Durham, I tend to like the city just the way it is, and support the feisty if futile efforts to protect it from powerful committees with grand visions. One particularly hard-fought battle occurred when the County Council, having been given a sizeable grant by the EU to improve the city, decided to spend it by moving

the equestrian statue of Lord Londonderry thirty yards from one end of the Market Square to the other. This created an enormous fuss: a huge campaign was mounted against the proposed move by the citizens of the county, who were perfectly happy with "the man on the horse" just where he was and resented him being shifted.

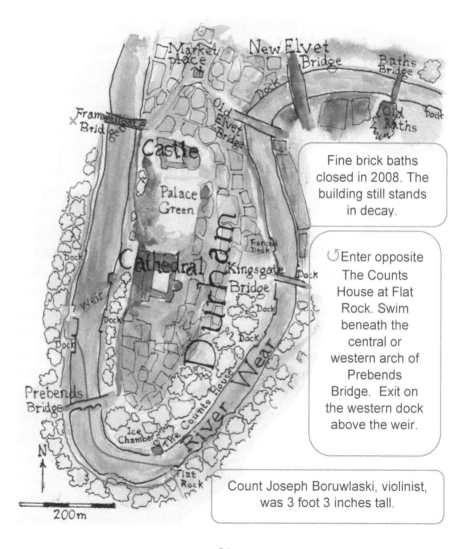

Fine brick baths closed in 2008. The building still stands in decay.

↺Enter opposite The Counts House at Flat Rock. Swim beneath the central or western arch of Prebends Bridge. Exit on the western dock above the weir.

Count Joseph Boruwlaski, violinist, was 3 foot 3 inches tall.

Furthermore, to move the statue, it was said, would bring bad luck to the city. The Council, when it realised the strength of feeling, became all the more determined to relocate the statue in order demonstrate that *it* was in charge. The whole city was convulsed for years over this, until in 2010 the statue was finally moved. It must have been a bit like Paris during the Dreyfus affair.

Hoping to raise the consciousness of the proletariat to a higher level, left-wing types tried to insert themselves into this bitter fight. They would go round telling people earnestly about how Lord Londonderry had been, a *very bad man*. Nobody took the *slightest notice*. They couldn't care less: they *liked* the statue of the man on the horse, and that was that.

The body of Saint Cuthbert
The man on the horse affair was not the first time there had been statue trouble in Durham. On the 31st of December 1540, the King's Commissioners marched into Durham Cathedral. Their purpose had to do with the one hundred and seven statues that adorned the great stone choir screen: they had come to smash them all. But the statues were gone; forewarned, the monks had spirited them away and to this day their location is a mystery. Perhaps the statues lie behind a bricked-up wall in the castle. Or perhaps they stand deep in one of the caves that riddle the Durham Dales, quietly awaiting discovery like the terracotta warriors of Xian.

Frustrated at the disappearance of the statues, the commissioners turned to their second object: the body of Cuthbert. The saint had died in 687 and for the next three hundred years his corpse—it is said—had been carried around the North by monks, until he was buried in Durham in 999. Just over a hundred years later, in 1104, Cuthbert was solemnly reburied in the newly built cathedral. The chroniclers of the time claimed that throughout this long period, Cuthbert's body had remained whole and uncorrupted, although the hard-headed commissioners did not believe this. All the more credible, therefore, are the contemporary reports that when the commissioners opened up the grave and tipped Cuthbert out of his coffin—breaking one of his legs—they found that he continued to be whole and uncorrupted, apart from his nose.

The body was reburied in 1545 and allowed to rest until 1827, when it was again dug up. On this occasion, it was perhaps rather disappointing to find that it had disintegrated in the usual way, so that all that was left was a skeleton. However, opinion is divided on the implications of this. Some argue that as the body uncovered in 1827 had plainly lain undisturbed since 1545, it *must have been* Cuthbert's body, which God had allowed to rot as a sign of his displeasure at its callous handling by the commissioners. On the contrary, others argue that it *could not* have been Cuthbert's body, because if it had have been, it would not have rotted. Around this second explanation have grown up any number of stories that the real body, like the statues, remains hidden. Some say that Cuthbert's body lies elsewhere in the vast cathedral, or at least that the building gives a clue as to its location. These stories include: the irregular pattern on the pillar by the clock; the third step to the tower; the discovery in 2013 of the message in the bottle, and— particularly popular amongst choir boys—the writing on the wall that is visible only at midsummer when the sun shines through a hole in the roof. Outside the cathedral are further possible clues. Hidden in the undergrowth of the surrounding woods are vaulted chambers; these so-called ice houses have the ostensible purpose of facilitating the production of ice cream and other chilled delicacies, but might this have been a cover for their real purpose: the preservation of Cuthbert's body? A few miles away is the Catholic seminary of Ushaw College: an enormous, magnificent hodge podge of buildings and the home of the ring found on Cuthbert's finger (if it *was* his finger)—what secrets might lie there? Or maybe knowledge of the place that the body has been secreted is held in one of the more notorious of the university colleges where, it is claimed, members of the senior common room perform unsavoury rites in a curtained hall lit by black candles. And then there is the Legend of the Three. An ancient note found sewn inside the lining of a waistcoat is one of several sources that attest to the existence of three men entrusted with the knowledge of Cuthbert's true location, with a new person chosen by the remining two each time someone dies.

What is to be made of all this? A moment's rational thought leads inevitably to the conclusion that those who claim that the body uncovered in 1827 was *not* that of Cuthbert are *quite right*, but for reasons that are *wholly wrong*. What we might call Cuthbert's official body is, obviously, really that of someone else because bodies inexorably decay so he could not have been whole, apart from his nose, in 1540 more than 800 years after his death. A fresh body must have been substituted, with the missing nose suggesting that 'Cuthbert' is probably a victim of syphilis, which was then ravaging Europe after being brought back from the New World by Columbus.

This reasoning, pursued further, suggests that this can hardly have been the first occasion on which 'Cuthbert's' body had been swapped. As Cuthbert was reported to have been whole and incorrupt when he was reinterred in the Cathedral in 1104, this body too must have been substituted. And then what of the preceding centuries when he was being carried around the North? The answer is inevitable: the body of the saint was constantly being changed for a new one.

But how, then, did the travelling monks reconcile themselves not only to (a) lying, but also to (b) the pointlessness of lugging about and venerating the wrong body? Here we are dealing with the motives of the human heart where nothing is certain. I would suggest, however, that the changing of the corpse was done quite openly, probably ceremoniously, to turn the new body into Cuthbert. The monks would have understood that one physical object—in this case a body—was as good as another as a symbol of their spiritual home. The passing onwards of some memento to a new body, perhaps the ring from one finger to the next, would be sufficient to impart the essence of Cuthbert. Just as the ordinary physical objects of bread and wine are said to become the flesh and blood of Jesus in the celebration of Eucharist, so an ordinary person's body could become that of a saint. Transferring Cuthbert from one cadaver to the next acknowledged that we are all equal in death. Ashes to ashes and dust to dust, our flesh crumbles but in spirit we will all become as pure as saints. This humanistic and egalitarian philosophy, however, was forgotten—or perhaps deliberately erased—being replaced by a very different doctrine of the virginal, miraculous, death-defying Cuthbert. It is this story that became fixed in the hagiography even as the body of the sixteenth century syphilitic beneath his shrine was slowly reclaimed by the earth.

2. Bainbridge

This swimhike explores Bainbridge and Askrigg in Wensleydale in the Yorkshire Dales. There was once a large Roman fort in the village. Now there are just bumps, defended by cows. In place of the fort, the route visits a nicely situated modern stone circle that lies in a rocky hollow west of Scar Top.

A statue of Commodus once stood in Bainbridge fort. He was a particularly evil and disgusting emperor who spent his time killing people for fun. Commodus renamed Rome after himself, renamed more or less everything of note after himself in fact, including statues of other people. He also had lots of statues of himself made, often presenting him in the guise of Hercules. But after he was assassinated, the Senate ordered that everything that Commodus had renamed, including all the statues, were to revert back to what they had been called before, and had Commodus' own statues smashed up. The statue at Bainbridge survived, however, and was dug up in the sixteenth century. It has since disappeared, but presumably, somewhere in Yorkshire, the last British monument to the vile tyrant still stares benignly down into someone's back garden.

℧ Enter the Ure at the stream below Yorebridge. In high water, you will also need to swim across at the stepping stones south of Askrigg. Enter from the stony beach 20 yards lower down to exit on small boulders.

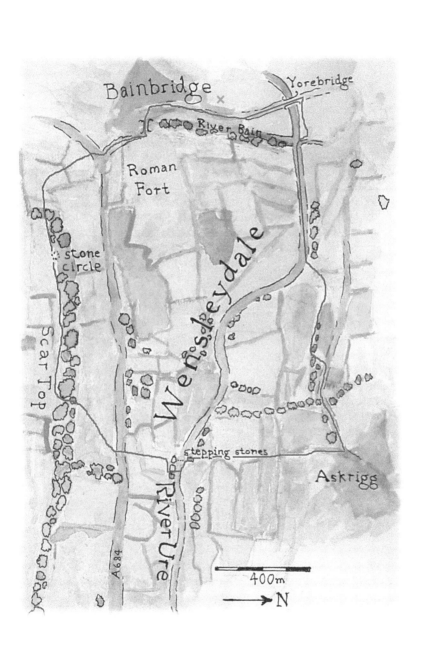

3. York

York Minster is in some ways even better than the cathedral at Durham because although it is not as big, it has far more surviving statues and carvings. Edging the choir in the Minster is the Kings' Screen, showing fifteen succeeding kings of England, starting with William the Conqueror. All of them look somewhat mad or decidedly wicked or both, apart from the last one, Henry VI. Henry looks nice, and perhaps he really was because after he was murdered by the next king, Edward IV—who was as wicked as all of the others—people started treating his statue as that of a saint. So it was taken down and destroyed and the plinth left empty, until a new one was carved in the nineteenth century.

The creation of statues to adorn the Minster continues to this day. Look up high amongst the grotesque gargoyles, and see the head of a respectable man wearing glasses. The streets of York are also fascinating; there are occasional carvings there too, especially of cats, as well as all kinds of interesting shops. My favourite, in a basement somewhere, is an enchanted antique shop selling roman coins and mermaids in formaldehyde. But as you tour the town, your eyes will doubtless be drawn to the River Ouse and you will be wondering: Can you swimhike there? Yes, you can. If you walk downriver to below the Millennium Bridge, there are several places to get in and out. However, the mapped swimhike is a good three miles upriver, so you may want to use wheels to get there, hopefully by cycling.

↺ Cycle Route 66 follows the Ouse north from York, bending away from the river just before a double rail bridge. Leave your bicycle at the plough seat and hike north up the bike trail, west along the road and south along the footpath to the Ouse. Swim east downriver to the bridge, *change into long trousers* and make your way back through the stinging nettles to your bike.

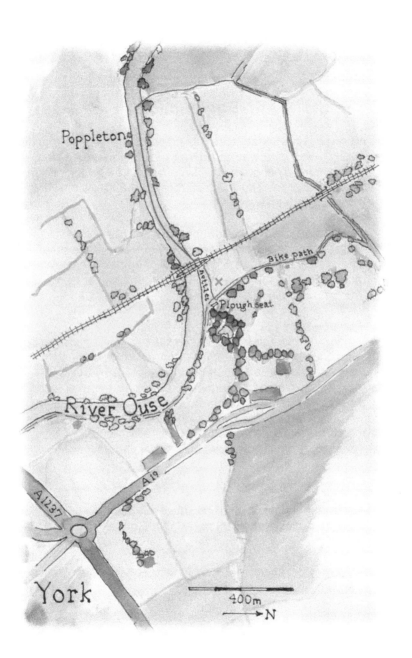

4. Egglescliffe

As the river Tees approaches Middlesbrough, its surrounding woods and fields give way to urban sprawl. However, before the countryside quite disappears, the Tees passes below the charming village of Egglescliffe. This is the starting point for a swimhike down a long stretch of deep water.

Egglescliffe sounds like a corruption of the adjacent village of Eaglescliffe. Etymologists, however, claim that it is the other way around and that eagles are a corruption of eggles, which refers to the Church (St John the Baptist) on top of the bank at Egglescliffe, as in the French *eglise*.

The disappearance of Leo
The fields south of Egglescliffe are the site of a mystery dating back to the Second World War. Leo, a religiously inclined conscientious objector, had become a labourer on the local farm. One day, he was part of a group hoeing turnips in a field by the river when he thought that he heard the voice of God calling him. Leo stopped, dropped his hoe, walked off with his arms in the air *and disappeared*. It is added that what Leo actually heard were the cries of the peacocks that lived across the river at Clock House.

There are three explanations for this story.

First—and in logic this cannot be ruled out even if it is felt to be extremely unlikely—Leo *was* called by God and ascended to Heaven.

Second, it may be, sadly, that in trying to reach the crying peacocks on the far bank, Leo drowned.

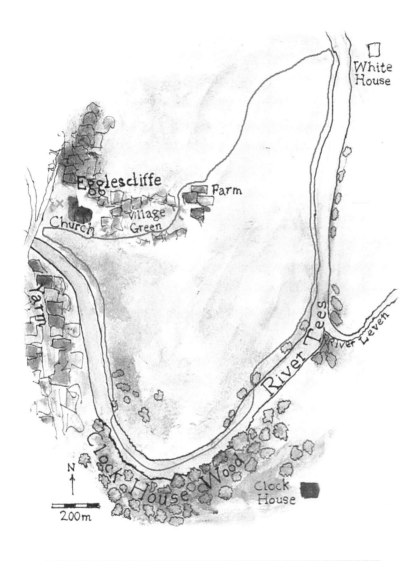

White House

Egglescliffe

Farm

Church

Village Green

Farm

River Tees

River Leven

Clock House Wood

Clock House

N

200m

↺Regular fishing platforms enable you to get in and out along the whole length of the river as is bends around Egglescliffe.

This second explanation, however, is even less satisfactory than the first. The beauty of a peacock, it is true, is so unearthly that to *see* one is to get a glimpse of heaven. However, the *cry* of the peacock is singularly ugly and unpleasant, so unpleasant, in fact, that it would be quite impossible to mistake it for the voice of God. It is far more likely, therefore, that Leo's fellow labourers in the turnip field—who may previously have *seen* but not *heard* the birds—mistook the voice of God for that of a peacock rather than Leo making the mistake the other way around.

Third, Leo entered the water, yes, but then got out again downstream, picked up the belongings that he had stowed beforehand, and continued his life elsewhere.

I tend towards this third intriguing possibility. Leo probably had an unhappy time in Egglescliffe and wanted to get away. The story shows a distinct lack of concern for what happened to him and the business about the peacocks rather suggests that he was made the butt of jokes. I also know, from my own family history, that being a conscientious objector in the Second World War could be hard, as my grandpa tried to be one. After three months of cleaning toilets, he decided he'd rather join the army and was shipped off to Singapore. (Those three months, however, were vital, as just before his troopship arrived, the city fell.) If Leo did decide to go AWOL, the looping geography of the river and the paths around the farm, mean that the Egglescliffe swimhike must more or less exactly follow the route that he took as he prepared to make a fresh start in life.

Peg Powler

The Tees is the home of Peg Powler, who lures men and boys into the water and to their deaths. She appears a beautiful woman in distress, but you can tell that she is, in fact, Peg Powler by her green hair. Peg Powler, then, is a freshwater siren or mermaid. Although mermaids are generally associated with the oceans, there is no reason why one should not come upriver from the North Sea in the same manner that seals sometimes do. And indeed, along the coast at Skinningrove a mere ten miles south of the mouth of the Tees, Camden notes the capture of a seaman (*Hominem marinum*) "who lived on raw fish some days; but at last taking his opportunity, he made his escape again into his own element." Camden adds that the ignorant fishermen there believe that the sea makes horrible gurgles when it is hungry, before swallowing them up.

The plausibility of this report lies first, in how Camden establishes his reliability as a narrator by dismissing the idea of the sea as an enormous monster; second, in his scientific classification of the seaman at the centre of the tale, and third in the prosaic nature of his description of what happened—without the faintest hint of the dark eroticism associated with mermaids. In the more familiar stories, mermaids sing bewitching songs to drive men mad with desire. Alternatively, the mermaid sits demurely on a rock combing her long hair in a mirror, apparently unconscious of the greedy eyes of watching mariners, that draw quietly in hoping to catch her, until their ship hits a reef. Then the mermaid laughs and dives under the water. Mermaids personify the ocean itself: a source of fascination, and yet at any moment liable to be of deadly danger. The alternative theory, that belief in mermaids was inspired by sightings of manatees or sea cows, is untenable. The homely features of these creatures bear not the slightest resemblance to those of a beautiful woman. Neither do manatees sing; they squeak.

5. Norwich

In Norwich cathedral, a misericord from the early fifteenth century shows a mermaid suckling a lion. Is this mermaid a seductress, tempting man to abandon reason and assume a bestial character that will end in his ruin?   It does not appear so.   The mermaid's musical conch shell and her mirror have both been set aside so that she can embrace the lion, who seems to be well settled and thoroughly enjoying himself.   Fortune is a woman, and *fortune favours the bold.*   It is the allusion to this motto as against the more familiar depiction of the mermaid as nemesis that makes the misericord so intriguing. For swimhikers, the mixed message is especially apt. The water needs no siren to call us in. And we know, sadly, of the tragedies that all too often occur in the rivers, lakes and seas where we swim. Yet we know too, of the sweet joy to be gained from them.

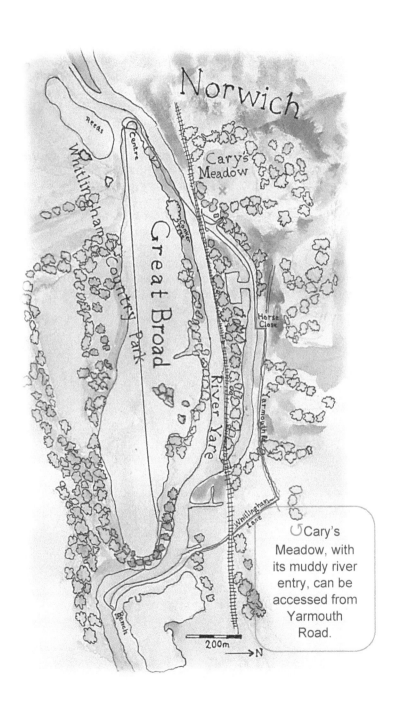

Norwich

Reeds

Whitlingham Country Park

Centre

Cary's Meadow

Goose Lane

Great Broad

River Yare

Horse Close

Yarmouth Rd

Whitlingham Lane

Bench

↺Cary's Meadow, with its muddy river entry, can be accessed from Yarmouth Road.

200m →N

About a mile from the cathedral, Great Broad in Whitlingham Country Park provides the sparkling centrepiece of a swimhike that also takes in the considerably less sparkly River Yare. The mud particles I stirred up on crawling out of the river were rather clingy and even after taking a shower I was still smelly. You may wish to adapt the route accordingly. Great Broad, however, is delightful.

When I swam along the lake, an enormous machine was sucking gravel through pipes at its eastern end. Possibly this machine might have been considered a health and safety hazard, but if so, it no longer matters because it has gone. Nonetheless, under 'Frequently Asked Questions' the park authorities state that "unfortunately" you are not allowed to swim in Great Broad, adding "If you would like to try open water swimming why not speak with Tri Anglia, they run regular training sessions in the Broad." For anyone hoping to enjoy swimming in Great Broad without subjecting themselves to the rigours of being trained by this particular triathlon club, no further information is supplied.

6. London

Hampstead Heath has three designated swimming ponds. The Men's Pond and Mixed Pond are peaceful tree lined places, and although I have never visited it, I expect the same is true of the Ladies' Pond.*

---

* There was some controversy in 2019 when the Corporation of London changed the admission rules for the Ladies' Pond to include those who had undergone a personal process of reassigning their sex, or who were at least proposing to do so. From a utilitarian perspective, something that might help to bring swimmers on both sides of the issue closer together is that in just about every other body of water in London, *no one at all* is allowed to swim, regardless of their sex. If more of these places were opened up, to mixed bathing, then everyone would benefit.

Whenever I visit London, I always seem to end up floating in one or other of these ponds, and when I do, I always have the same thought-sequence, which goes like this:

"This is *lovely*," I think to myself dreamily as I drift around on my back. "It is so *unlike* London. It is as though I could *really be* out in the countryside. Look! They've even got *coots!*" Then I roll over with a jerk. "Hold on! What am I *doing* here? If the countryside is so nice and London is not, why *aren't* I in the countryside? Why am I in London *at all?*"

I have never really found a satisfactory answer to this question, which is why I have stopped visiting London, unless dragged there by my wife.

You can, of course, combine swimming in the Hampstead ponds with a walk around the Heath, but this is swimming and hiking rather than swimhiking as you get in and out of the water at one spot. So, I tried the Serpentine in Hyde Park. I had ventured into the green water of the Serpentine before, developed a painful ear infection, and vowed never to swim there again, but that had been several years earlier. If I kept my head up doing breaststroke that would surely be alright.

It is early when I arrive, but already a posse of swimmers are walking down to the eastern end of the lake. I follow them through a little gate to the water's edge, where there is a man with a clipboard.

Peter: [friendly Little Noddy voice] Hello! Is this a race?
Man with Clipboard: Yes.
Peter: [immediately forgetting resolution not to put head in the water] Can I join in?
Man with Clipboard: No.
Peter: Oh. Well, perhaps I can just swim from here then?
Man with Clipboard: No. Only members of the Serpentine Swimming Club are allowed to swim in the Serpentine.

I go down to the other end of the lake and find a buoyed off area that is set aside for swimming.

Woman: Excuse me! You can't walk through there.
Peter: I'm just going to have a swim in this bit, so as not to get in the way of the competition.
Woman: Are you a member of the club?
Peter: Me? Yes. But *[deprecating laugh]* I'm afraid I am far too slow to join in with the race.

So I swim around in the buoyed off area. It is all rather galling. Being policed by the police is one thing, being policed by your fellow swimmers is quite another. But it was my fault: I should have simply ignored them.

When Health Secretary Matt Hancock was pictured in an embrace with a woman-who-was-not-his-wife, the public was terribly shocked, because lovers' trysts *were against covid rules.* So he had to resign. With more time on his hands, Mr Hancock went jogging in Hyde Park and took a spontaneous dip in the Serpentine, where he had a broadly similar experience to mine. Once again Matt Hancock had broken the rules. This time, however, he fought back, declaring that the Serpentine should be free for anyone to swim in. And quite right too. There are some occasions when rules, however sound in the main, should be broken. There are even occasions when what is shocking is not that the rules have been broken, but that they were ever obeyed in the first place.

7. Chertsey

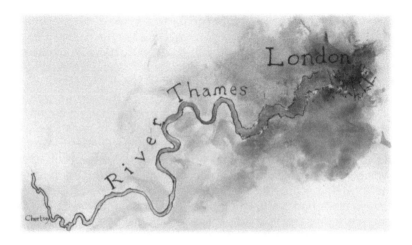

If you look down into the Thames in central London, it glares back at you large, dirty, dangerous and forbidding. Various people have swum across it nonetheless, including Matthew Parris and his friend Jonathan, so a swimhike is obviously possible. However, I am too cowardly to attempt it and I advise you to be the same. Instead of risking your life in London let us travel about 20 miles upstream, to Chertsey, where the feeling is wholly different. Here the river is smaller, and so much more inviting you would hardly think it possible that this same waterway sloshes through the capital. So I found it, early on a serene summer's morning; it is a safe and pleasant spot to go swimhiking.

Sheltered by Dumsey Meadow and Chertsey Meads, the town of Chertsey has had some protection from the urban sprawl created by grasping developers, and back in the seventeenth century, when it was surrounded by common meadows, it must have been idyllic and certainly a far nicer place to live than the plague-ridden capital. It is hardly surprising, therefore, that the poet Abraham Cowley took ownership of one of these meadows as a 'nest egg' and retired to the town in 1665. Poor Cowley, though, could never harvest any

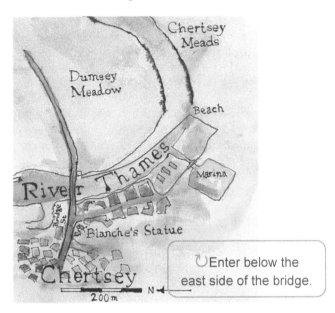

grass from his meadow as it was "eaten up every night by cattle put in by my neighbours." It must have been terribly frustrating. Then, in July 1667, the poet made the fatal error of walking in his meadow late in the evening, presumably to put a stop to these incursions. The grass was *damp* and the result was all too predictable: Cowley caught a cold and two weeks later he was dead. Chertsey's most famous historical personage, however, is not Cowley; it is Blanche Heriot.

After the defeat of the Lancastrians in the 1471 Battle of Tewkesbury, Neville Audley was captured by Yorkists in Chertsey, and was about to be put to death when he claimed that the new King Edward IV would pardon him, or at least that he *might*. His captors agreed that Audley could send a messenger to the King in London to see what he had to say on the matter, but added that if they had not heard back by the time that the curfew bell was rung at Chertsey Abbey the following night, they would kill him anyway. The next night fell and the messenger had not returned. But as the executioners awaited the tolling of the bell, Audley's beloved, Blanche Heriot, climbed the tower of the Abbey and clung on to its clapper, preventing the bell from sounding. At this point, the tardy messenger turned up, made some feeble excuse about being late because of his horse, and presented a Royal Pardon. Neville was released, married Blanche, and they all lived happily ever after.

With the eager virtue that characterises the hunters of 'misinformation', this story is nowadays flagged as a fake, invented in the 1840s by Albert Smith. Smith, however, claimed to have set down what he had heard as oral history, and who is to say he didn't? In any event, when a developer wanted to put up a large and unappealing modern office block in the heart of the ancient and historic town, he was told—what a cunning ruse!—that he would *only* be allowed to do so *if he also paid for a statue of Blanche stilling the bell.* The developer agreed; he got his office block and the joyous townsfolk got their statue.

In the statue (at the start of the route by the bridge) Blanche stands pulling the clapper. In Smith's story she actually leaps on to the clapper and holds herself to it, like a horse in a merry-go-round, as she gets bashed backwards and forwards inside the bell. But, however she did it, Blanche Heriot is a great heroine, and if she is indeed fictional, at least there will be no secrets in her closet that will end up with her statue being torn down and chucked in the river.

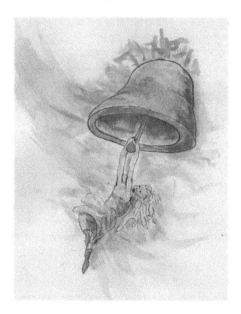

Jersey

8. Portelet Bay

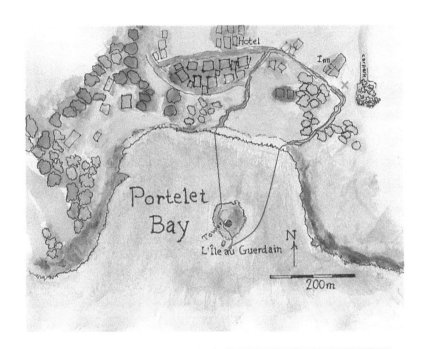

↺ L'Ile au Guerdain, also known as Janvrin's Tomb, can also be visited on foot at low tide. The tower on the island was built in 1808 to guard against Napoleon.

Portelet Bay is the site of a terrible accident. Eight boys on a school picnic trip drowned there in July 1915.

We went to Jersey on a whim, out of season. Doubtless, there are normally lots of things to do there, but when we visited most of them were shut, apart from Gerald Durrell's zoo. As a child I was entranced by Durrell's books about growing up in Corfu and then going off to Africa to catch animals. The zoo, however, was rather ordinary, which was somehow disillusioning. Still, I at least had grand swimhiking plans. But then, after emerging from the sea on my very first swimhiking trip, to L'Ile au Guerdain in Portelet Bay on the southwest side of the island, I discovered that my dry bag's seam had ripped and everything in the swimsac was soaking wet. So this is the only route I did.

On the day we left, we found there was somewhere else to go. It was a place that we had previously somehow missed and, as luck would have it, we just had time to see it before getting back to the airport. So we went to Devil's Hole, with its large and grimly realistic statue of a brooding Satan, the embodiment of evil. The sight terrified our young son Nicholas.

Had we but realised it, our visit to Devil's Hole had set in motion some strange alchemy, one that privileged us with a rare glimpse into the future, when young people of Nicholas' generation would take very poorly to *bad* statues. But we *didn't* realise this, and so we tried just to laugh the whole thing off. Of course, this did not work. Nicholas spent the whole time on our return plane journey loudly proclaiming that we were all going to die. All things considered, I was glad to get back to England.

England Again

9. Bristol

On 7 June 2020, the statue of the philanthropic slave trader Edward Colston was pulled down by the crowd and thrown into Bristol Harbour, where it sank with a satisfying plop. Over the course of that troubled summer such attacks spread until it seemed that no statue was safe, unless they happened to be Nelson Mandela.

Colston's lynching followed riots over Confederate monuments in the USA, which had never been free of controversy. However, it represented something of a departure for the British, who had previously tended to regard statues as picturesque additions to parks and squares, with no more thought to who they might depict than if they were an old tree or, as in Durham, simply a man on a horse. But let Youth lead the way! The iconoclastic enthusiasm of our young people in striking a blow against seventeenth century slavery is to be applauded. I suppose—just possibly—that the current exploitation of thousands of undocumented migrants might be of more immediate concern. However, maybe they will sort that out next, and anyway even these people will no doubt feel much better about their lot in life once they are no longer oppressed by the presence of all these statues.

Some years before these events, I visited Bristol Harbour to see my friend Julie, who lives there. The harbour provides a diverting mixture for strollers: trendy eateries, flowery houseboats, speedboats, ferries, tall ships for the harbour festival, rowing boats, train tracks, a giant crane, an old ship built by Brunel and brought back from the Falklands, another old ship in dry dock, a real working shipyard you can walk through, and a succession of boats plying up and down. At eight o'clock the next morning, however, all is quiet, apart from the yellow ferry. I let this by, then descend the stone steps by Poole's Wharfe and start to breaststroke across the harbour, my swimsac on my back.

I am swimming at an angle to head for a little area that passes as a beach. Half way across, however, a great a commotion breaks out on the jetty near my exit. Shouts; running feet; urgency; a boat is launched.

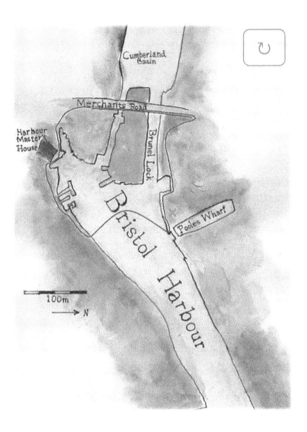

"Oh No! They're coming to rescue me!" I think.*

I change course, beelining for the far bank and Julie, who was watching, says I notably speeded up. I find a gap between two

---

* As readers of the second edition of *Swimhiking in the Lake District and North East England* will know, boats are *always* trying to rescue me.

moored boats and heave myself out, just in time to have prevented myself from being saved. Phew!

The 'rescue' boat swings into the gap at my landing place. It has 'Harbour Master' written on it.

"What was all that about?" asks the Harbour Master, a young man with a beard. He seems cross.

Peter: I was just having a swim.
Harbour Master: You can't go swimming in here. It's not allowed.
Peter: [So! The Harbour Master was not coming to rescue me after all, but to catch me.] Oh.
Harbour Master: There are various forms of traffic.
Peter: [And yet I got across! Ha Ha Ha!] Ah.
Harbour Master: There are occasional pollution issues.
Peter: Oh dear.
Harbour Master: There are varying depths.
Peter: Hmm.
Harbour Master: There are no swimming signs posted at various places around the harbour, that you are not *[he politely concedes]* necessarily expected to see *[though of course I had]*.
Peter: Are there?
Harbour Master: Are you a local?
Peter: No, I live in Durham. I'm here on holiday.
Harbour Master: [suspicious] Where are you going *now*?
Peter: Just a walk.
Harbour Master: A walk? *[still suspicious]* Will you give me an undertaking not to enter the water again?"
Peter: Yes, alright.
Harbour Master: [starting to pull away] Just over there, is a perfectly good *bridge* you can walk across."
Peter: But it's more fun to swim.

He does no deign to answer.

In such circumstances swimhiking really shows its worth. On a crossing such as this you can get in and, if you are quick, be safely out again on the far side before anyone can do anything about it, whereas if you had left your clothes on the bank while swimming around in the water, you are a sitting target.

As for the Harbour Master, he struck me as a responsible and reasonable young man but—I mused as I continued on—did he have the *authority* to ban swimhiking across the harbour? I mean, a car park attendant could hardly ban someone from crossing a road that happened to run through his car park, and how was this any different? Then, I remembered triumphantly that there are special rules in England pertaining to estuaries, where you have a legal right of access. I started rather regretting not raising this subject with him, but now I am glad I didn't, because, as Julie pointed out, Bristol Harbour has not been an estuary for some time. It was altered in the early nineteenth century to become a 'floating harbour'—essentially a lake.

10. Warwick

Warwick Castle is the ancestral home of the Nevilles, the king-makers. They lurk in all of Shakespeare's historical plays, and so they might as for several hundred years every strategic marriage, every battle and every double-crossing, somehow involves a Neville. But now they are gone and if you visit Warwick Castle you will find that you are accompanied everywhere by piped music, rather as though you were in a giant elevator. The head of Merlin Entertainment—which owns the place—apparently loves the music, and demands that it is switched up every time he visits. And because he might, like Saddam Hussein with one of his palaces, pop in unannounced at any time, the staff dare not switch the wretched stuff off. But this aside, the Castle is pretty good, albeit very expensive to visit for anyone aged three years and above. You can climb the spiral staircase to the tower, walk the walls, and see peacocks. You can doze on the artificial island created by Capability Brown, where JMW Turner painted his view of the castle and river. Unusually for the great artist, the scene did not include any boats. Sight-seeing boats irritated the castle's owners, so they deliberately had the island placed there to make the Avon too shallow for them. Above the island, you can visit the mill and see the wheels, the long leather loops connecting them made from giraffe necks. Looking upriver from the castle windows, to where the Avon is deeper, you can see paddle boats meandering about shaped as large plastic swans and flamingos. And a little further up from there is a short circular swimhike, one that roughly follows the boundaries of St. Nicholas Park.

On entering the park to recce the route on a warm summer's evening, I am delighted to see a sign displaying a green swimmer symbol. This is a first! But it turns out that it refers only to the indoor leisure pool, and soon I see the all too familiar red no swimming notices lining the banks of the Avon, signs that are being resolutely ignored by the children of Warwick. The children appear to be following a tradition of longstanding: a bench by the river commemorates a man who lived a lad here all his life, swimming in the river.

Castle

Eastgate

Gerrards

River

Castle Bridge

Avon

Myton Fields

Church

Warwick

St Nicholas Park

A445

Bike Trail

Sea Scout HQ

Kingfisher Pond

200m ⟶N

Next morning, I enter the water at the Sea Scout HQ, which has a handy concrete slipway into the water. Quickly, the river becomes deep, perfect for a gentle swim downriver, with willow trees, swans guarding their cygnets, a kingfisher. The exit, at Myton Field boat dock, is a convenient place to start exploring the picturesque streets of Warwick.

In the grounds of St Nicholas Church, a tree is planted in memory of Reverend Arthur Savage Wade, who fought for the freedom of all working men. What more is known of Rev Wade? From contemporary accounts I have only been able to find out three things: that he was a chartist (who wanted all men to have the vote rather than just a few of them), that he was overweight, and that he was lazy. No doubt it is true that Rev Wade was a chartist, but are either of the other two facts correct, or are they just bourgeois propaganda?

The swimhike ends with a walking loop of Kingfisher Pond. A sign warns that to steal tadpoles from the pond is strictly forbidden by the Wildlife and Countryside Act. What the children of Warwick make of this sign, I do not know.

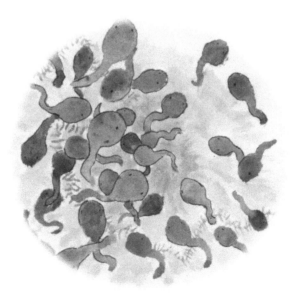

12. Leamington Spa

The Pump Room at Leamington opened in 1814 and its therapeutic pools, Turkish baths and swimming baths continued to be used until 1990, when they were closed. But not to worry, a notice was stuck on the door redirecting swimmers to the Newbold Comyn Leisure Centre—a venue that is no doubt very UpToDate, even if it may not have quite the same ambience. This, however, is not the only other option available, as starting from the Pump Room, you can instead take a figure of eight swimhiking route down the river Leam, where the very murkiness of the water suggests that it must surely contain the same curative properties that attracted visitors to the Spa.

The Grand Union Canal runs between Leamington Spa and Warwick, and shortly after the Leam joins the Avon, the canal crosses the river via an aqueduct. Using the canal in combination with the rivers seems to offer all kinds of swimhiking possibilities. But after peering down at it, I decided otherwise: the water was just too soupy.

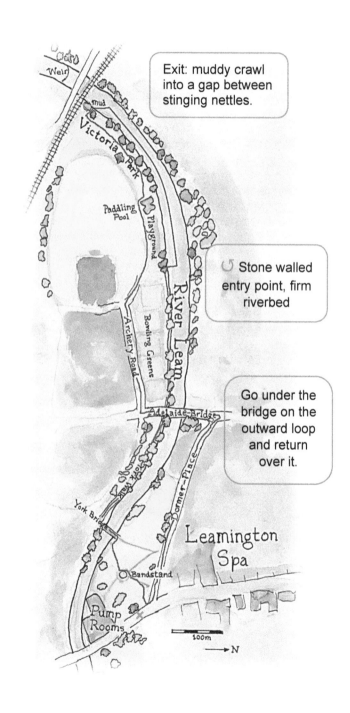

Exit: muddy crawl into a gap between stinging nettles.

Stone walled entry point, firm riverbed

Go under the bridge on the outward loop and return over it.

Weir

mud

Victoria Park

Paddling Pool

Playground

River Leam

Archery Road

Bowling Greens

Adelaide Bridge

Cormer Place

York Bridge

Leamington Spa

Bandstand

Pump Rooms

100m

N

12. Staveley

View near Potter Tarn

A circular swimhike starting from Staveley visits three lakes: Skeggles Water, quiet and beautiful; Gurnal Dubs, which is lovely for swimming, and Potter Tarn, which is perfectly fine but slightly disappointing after the other two. The best way round, therefore, might be to set off along the field footpath that goes straight up over the hill towards Potter Tarn, so as to cross it first. I did it the other way, heading towards Skeggles Water up a long dead-end road.

At the gate where the road from Staveley ended and the track began, a poem was pinned. One of the surprising but welcome side effects of the covid pandemic was the burst of creativity that flowered in its early weeks and months in the spring of 2020 when—lockdowns permitting—people would go out and place 'NHS stones', as well as poems and other artistic creations, along paths all over the country. These painted stones etc, usually complimented the staff of the National Health Service but sometimes also paid tribute to people like cleaners and delivery drivers who, we had suddenly realised, were so valuable to our day to day lives. Later, the stones and other artifacts stopped appearing, and indeed started to vanish.* So a year on, I was pleased to find that after most people had long since given up on the thing and gone back to dropping litter etc, that someone had shared their poem on the gate, and stopped to read it.

The poem was written from the perspective of a sheep, and was mainly taken up with graphic descriptions of what hikers' dogs could do to pregnant ewes, although the sheep also suggested that the hikers might be leaving trails of covid to infect her master. No wonder, the sheep concluded, that the master could be grumpy towards walkers he found on his land. I did not have a dog, and I was as sure as I could be that I did not have covid either as my friend Julie, in whose cottage I was staying, had asked that I take a test as a precaution. Even so, given the tone of the poem, I did not feel especially keen to meet its author.

The path is empty, but then, coming the other way, are two dogs. They appear quite friendly, until more arrive and they all turn into a pack. Soon there are about seven of them running round me barking, darting forward and back. I am not too concerned; it is all just show. Finally, the owner comes stumping down, waving his stick and shouting incomprehensible commands at them. No. It is not *them* he is shouting at; it is *me*.

Dog Owner: Put your map down! Put your map down! If you put your map up like that, or use a stick *[I don't have a stick]*, they'll attack you.
Peter: Will they?
Dog Owner: [offended] "Of course! If you threaten them, they'll be on you!"
Peter: I'd better watch out for them then.
Dog Owner: [as if I had just insulted his mother] Pardon?!

I repeat what I said, and the dog owner marches on muttering imprecations about walkers. Then, as I too continue on my way, he turns to shout them at me. Still, the dogs turned out to be friendly enough.

---

* I am mystified as to where the NHS stones all went—were they reclaimed by their creators, gently buried under leaves, pinched as garden ornaments?

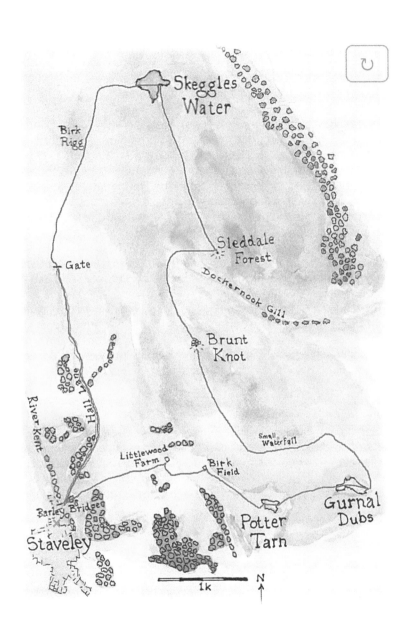

Skeggles Water

Birk Rigg

Sleddale Forest

Dockernook Gill

Gate

Brunt Knot

River Kent

Hall Lane

Small Waterfall

Littlewood Farm

Birk Field

Gurnal Dubs

Barley Bridge

Potter Tarn

Staveley

1k

N

I was left wondering whether I had met the poet. On the one hand this seemed very unlikely as: (a) he had a large number of dogs, who were (b) all off a lead and not under the slightest control. This is exactly the kind of thing that the poem objected to. But on the other hand: (c) his pungent comments about walkers implied that *he* was not one, and (d) he was certainly grumpy.

Staveley is as close as this book gets to the Lake District. Numerous routes in this wonderful area are described in *Swimhiking in the Lake District and North East England.* These swimhikes include the Frog Graham Round, the challenge course I completed in 2005. A few years later, the Round started to attract interest. Now, well over one hundred people have done it and there is a club to record their achievements. In one way this is gratifying, of course, but in another, it is irritating because I keep thinking:

"Why am I famous only for *this*? Why *[to take just once example]* am I *not* famous for my refutation of Einstein's theory of relativity?"[*]

Once the Frog Graham Round got going, my inability to deal with it soon became apparent. Fortunately, fell runner Martyn Price and long distance swimmer Richard Walsh volunteered to form the nucleus of a small but highly effective club committee. Matt Bland of Pete Bland Sports, a family business, also stepped in to support the club.

Pete Bland himself died of covid in 2020. Alongside his distinguished record as a fell runner and race organiser, Pete is remembered by generations of grateful fell runners for fitting them with exactly the kind of shoes they needed, first from the back of his van and later from his Kendal shop. He is commemorated by a bench in Staveley.

---

[*] See 'The Ideology of Relativity...'*Social Epistemology*, 2009, and 'Popper's response to Dingle...', *Studies in History and Philosophy of Modern Physics*, 2010. The argument that theoretical physicists have gone blundering off in the wrong direction and that they need to stop, take stock of the map, and retrace their steps, has attracted a *bit* of attention, mainly in the form of derision, although one or two physicists have contacted me privately to say that they agree. However, the only people who have publicly endorsed it are—in the eyes of the scientific establishment—cranks: to be treated as the butt of jokes and kept out of all the journals.

Scotland

Cairn at Loch Craig

Scotland is still part of Britain, at least for now, but feels increasingly distinct. It has its own laws which, much more so than in England, recognise our right to peacefully enjoy the countryside on both land and water. However, this autonomy has its downside, as in order to show how separate it is from England, Scotland introduced particularly draconian covid rules. Although most are now withdrawn, its government has threatened, at any time, to bring them back. Scotland is also doubly dangerous because as well as mermaids it has kelpies, horses that tempt you to sit on their back and then rush into the nearest loch to drown you.

13. Loch Skeen

Looking through my list of swimhikes, I feel I do not have *quite* enough in Scotland. So, in January 2022, I visit Loch Skeen, which has lain undisturbed—at least by me—over many a lazy hot summer's day. Still, the weather is clear, light snow has given a beautiful dusting to the hills, and clusters of sparkling icicles hang down from the grass. The swimhike involves a dogleg, but as this one runs up and down the Grey Mare's Tail waterfall, it is a particularly nice section to do twice.

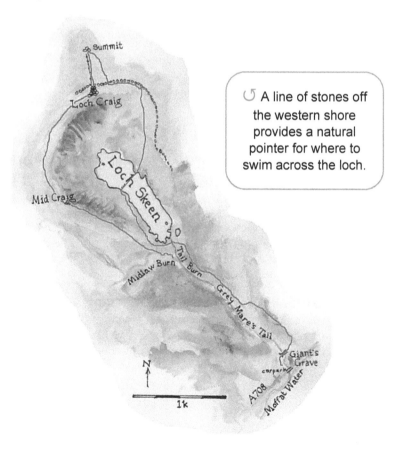

↺ A line of stones off the western shore provides a natural pointer for where to swim across the loch.

After getting back, I phone my father Mike to tell him that I have completed the last swimhike of the book. (My father likes to keep up with the outdoor activities of his children as he himself was once an elite fell runner, orienteer, cyclist and triathlete.)

Peter: Hello Dad. It's me. Peter. I've been swimhiking across Loch Skeen, near Moffat. Do you know it?

Mike: I might have done a mountain marathon there once... *[thinks]* Is it a *long* one?

Peter: Yes, quite long.

Mike: Yes, I might have been there. Were you in a wetsuit?

Peter: Yes.

Mike: And you swam its length of course.

Peter: No. I swam across it. You see, I'm writing my book now, but I didn't think I'd done enough about Scotland and so I thought I'd better do another.

Mike: I see. Not enough about Scotland in your book. You've swam across the Firth of Forth I suppose?

Peter: No.

Mike: [surprised and taken aback] The Tay?

Peter: No.

Mike: Loch Ness? *[making excuses for me in advance]* I suppose swimming the length of Loch Ness is rather a long way.

Peter: No, I haven't done Loch Ness, and actually swimming *across* Loch Ness might be a bit tough for me these days.

Mike: Loch Lomond?

Peter: No.

Mike: [desperately] The Trossachs? You *must* have been swimhiking in the Trossachs.

Peter: No. I haven't been there either.

Mike: Well Peter, what kind of a book *is* this?

14. Glen Trool

The Gaelic names that adorn the Scottish mountains have a wild poetry about them, but once the initial thrill of rolling them around your tongue has worn off, they start to become somewhat repetitive and, if you look up what they mean, dully descriptive as yet another Beinn Mhor (Big Hill) Beinn Bhreac (Speckled Hill),or Beinn Bhreac Mhor (Big Speckled Hill) turns up. It was, therefore, with especial pleasure that I pored over the map of Galloway while planning a swimhike. Here were names that really were darkly romantic! Murder Hole, Awful Hand, Wolf Slock, Rig of the Jarkness. What terrible stories might lie behind them? However, it appears that some of these names may be of recent origin, and that the small round bay called Murder Hole in particular, was appropriated from a river pool some miles to the west merely to suit the convenience of the nineteenth century novelist SR Crockett. Still, Glen Trool really does have a murderous history, with graves in the valley to the Scottish covenantors, surprised and killed there in 1685. Also, in 1307 there was the Battle of Glen Trool, which marked the turning point in Robert the Bruce's campaign to become King of Scotland, after he had been forced to hide all winter in a cave with a spider. At least the Scots *claim* that there was a battle there, and that Robert the Bruce won, and have built a sizeable monument on the site to prove it, although by the English account all that happened was that Bruce crept up and quietly stole some of their horses.

The swimhike I planned, The Six Lochs of Glen Trool, looked great on the map and no doubt it is very beautiful on the ground, although I cannot say an awful lot more, as when I finally had the chance to complete it, it was misty all day. As well as seeing next to nothing of the countryside, I also saw nobody, although on the approach to Loch Enoch I was stalked by two goats: large, devilish, shaggy brown coats, long horns. However, somebody else was there with me because on the top of Merrick they had placed a large red apple. It looked delicious and yet whoever had carried it up there had only eaten a small part. They had gnawed around the edge of the apple, biting off the skin to reveal the succulent flesh beneath. But then they had stopped, leaving the exposed flesh looking entirely white and fresh, as though the eater had left off not more than a minute before I arrived. There is only one path up and down Merrick and as I ran down it, I was hoping to meet them and have a chat. But, as I say, I saw no one.

15. Loch Dee

Loch Dee is in a quiet area of the Scottish countryside and much of this route is off-track. However, tiny paths—very satisfying to follow—run between the south shore of Loch Dee and near Dr Borthwick's seat, and between Curleywee and Bennanbrack.

The area is little explored partly because of the difficulties of the terrain. One would think that the higher you climbed a mountain, the harder it would get. In fact, the ground, on average, gets harder to traverse the lower you are. Up high there is grass, low heather and stones that are all relatively easy to cross, while lower down there are an exhausting series of great tussocks and tall heather that scratches your legs.

Sawny Bean
Where was the cave of the cannibal Sawny Bean? SR Crockett, places it simultaneously by the sea and in the vicinity of Bennanbrack. As with Murder Hole, Crockett may have been taking liberties with geography, because the generally accepted location of the cave is on the coast some 20 miles west of the mountain. However, not a single human bone has ever been found in this cave, raising doubts that Bean was there, or even existed at all. Crockett was born and raised in Galloway. Did he learn through oral traditions of a location that contradicted the cave's 'official' spot? Maybe we have been looking in the wrong place. Rather than having his lair by the shore, did Bean spy down from a mountain outcrop at the pass between Glenhead and Loch Dee? Was it here that he would approach travellers by stealth in the mist before deciding whether to advance and invite his prey to dinner or make silent retreat? Perhaps somewhere, still undiscovered on the bleak craggy slopes of Bennanbrack, is a hideout strewn with bones.

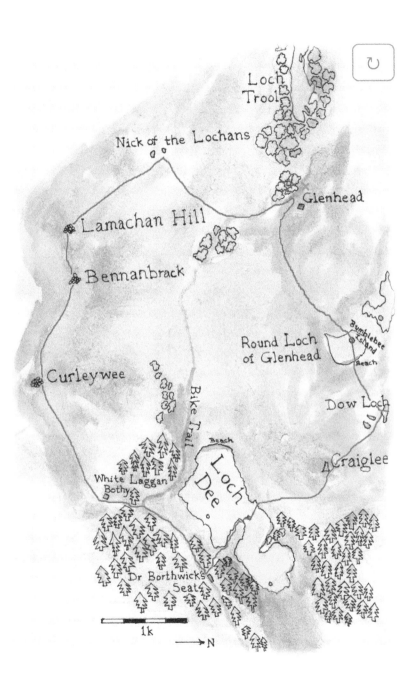

Wales

Glaslyn and Llyn Llydaw from the Miners' Track

Wales, like Scotland, has aspirations to independence. It might be objected that in Wales' case in particular, it really is just too small to be an independent country. But then, what does size have to do with the rightness or wrongness of the matter? I once supervised a PhD student who argued that everybody, down to the owners of a one bedroom flat, had a right to secede from the country of which they were a part and to form their own independent state.

16. Snowdonia

This swimhike follows The Miners' Track, one of the popular paths that leads up towards Snowdon, crossing two of the lakes that are met along the way. It then takes another popular path, the Pyg Track, back down. Above the Pyg Track is another path along Crib Goch, a knife edge ridge. If you follow *this* path, you will either (a) love it, or (b) find it terrifying and vow never to do it again. I have only done it once. I should also mention that unless you are a lot more organised than me, it will be impossible to park your car at the starting point at Pen-y-pass, so you will either have to extend the route, or take a shuttle bus or, best of all, not have a car with you in the first place.

What is particularly pleasing about this swimhike is that where the two paths converge, instead of continuing up the dogleg to the top of Snowdon, like everyone else is doing, *you simply go back down again*. I owe this excellent and insightful route choice to my son, Nicholas, who worked it out when aged just six. We were doing the hike as a family and when we finally reached the junction, already quite late in the day, my wife Toshie and I got summit fever.

"Come on!" we said. 'We've still just got time! It's not far now. Let's go for it!"
"Why?" asked Nicholas. "Why don't we just go back?"

We dragged him on up for a bit and then realised that he was actually quite right, and turned around. The deeper wisdom of Nicholas' route choice, however, was not impressed upon me until many years later, until autumn 2021 in fact, when Toshie and I took the same route again. This time we *did* go to the top, and when we got there, we had to stand in the cold in a queue for a good ten minutes to wait for our turn to touch the topmost cairn. Now, when people go up a mountain, they have to take a photograph to prove it. This is no longer simply a desire that people feel, it is a necessity; if they do not take a photo, what they have done *does not really exist*. The problem on Snowdon—at least I think it is a problem—is

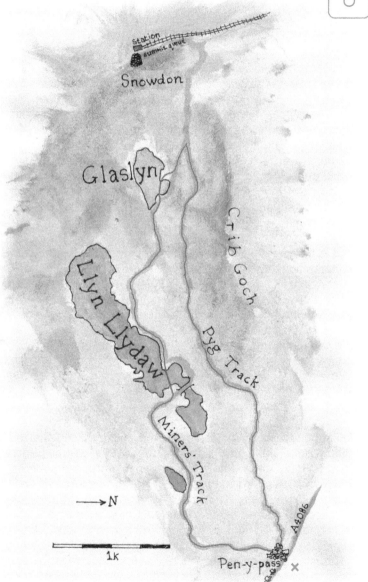

that a convention has developed that not only must you have your photo taken on the top, but that you must also be the only person there; it is not good enough to have your picture taken in a kind of scrum, you have to appear to be in splendid isolation. So, we stood in the queue and waited our turn.

I was annoyed about this, and what made me even more grumpy was how patient and good humoured everyone else in the queue was. They did not moan about the cold and the wind. When people ahead in the queue slowly and cautiously crawled up the final rocks to the summit instead of walking up them, they did not roll their eyes. When a group on the summit seemed to want to take an endless series of pictures of every combination of people from every angle, they did not grind their teeth and tear their hair. And then, when someone chose the top of Snowdon not only to pose for a photograph, but also to propose marriage—which naturally slowed things down even more—my own anguished cries of "Oh Gawd! Whatever next!" were drowned out by their delighted applause.

My nephew Daniel told me I was lucky. *His* photo on Snowdon, taken in good weather in the summer, showed a queue that stretched interminably down the mountain into the distance.

"How long did you queue for?" I asked him.
"Oh, we didn't. We just stood around on the flat bit just below the final rocks. We thought that that would do for the summit."

But *does* this do? *Has* Daniel in fact been to the top of Snowdon? I have been deeply schooled in the view that to reach the top of a mountain you have to touch *the topmost cairn,* otherwise it *does not count.* (I have, indeed, been quite pedantic about this in the Frog Graham Round Club.) But then, what *could* Daniel do? The dilemma seems insoluble. It would be *silly* to queue for hours, but it would be *rude* to push in. So, as I say, I am particularly pleased with the way that the swimhiking route recommended here manages to avoid the problem altogether.

17. The Rhinogs

Paths in the Rhinogs are rare and the open ground can make for rough going. The rake up Carreg-y-Saeth is particularly tricky (and would be even harder to come down). I feel slightly apologetic, therefore, that the swimhike that goes between the three lakes takes you across rather than along one of the few good paths that there are, the Roman Steps.

The Roman Steps, so-called, were not in fact put there by the Romans, but were constructed as a packhorse route in the medieval period. At least this is what everybody says, with great confidence, although I do not know how they are so sure—would steps really help a packhorse? The line of the steps, it is true, is not as straight as one would expect of a Roman road, and the Roman style of doing things was remarkable for its uniformity throughout their vast domain. But the steps are not that bendy either. In this remote location at the very edge of the empire and hidden from view by the surrounding mountains, is it not possible that a Roman engineer, admiring the sinuous art of the Celts, thought it might go unremarked if the path was built to be just a *bit* curvy?

1. ↺ **Three lakes** Dinas → Pont Crafnant → Gloyw Lyn → Llyn Du → Llyn Morwynion → Cwm Bychan → Dinas

2. ↻ **Carreg-y-Saeth** Dinas → Llyn Cwm Bychan → Carreg-y-Saeth → Pont Crafnant→ Dinas

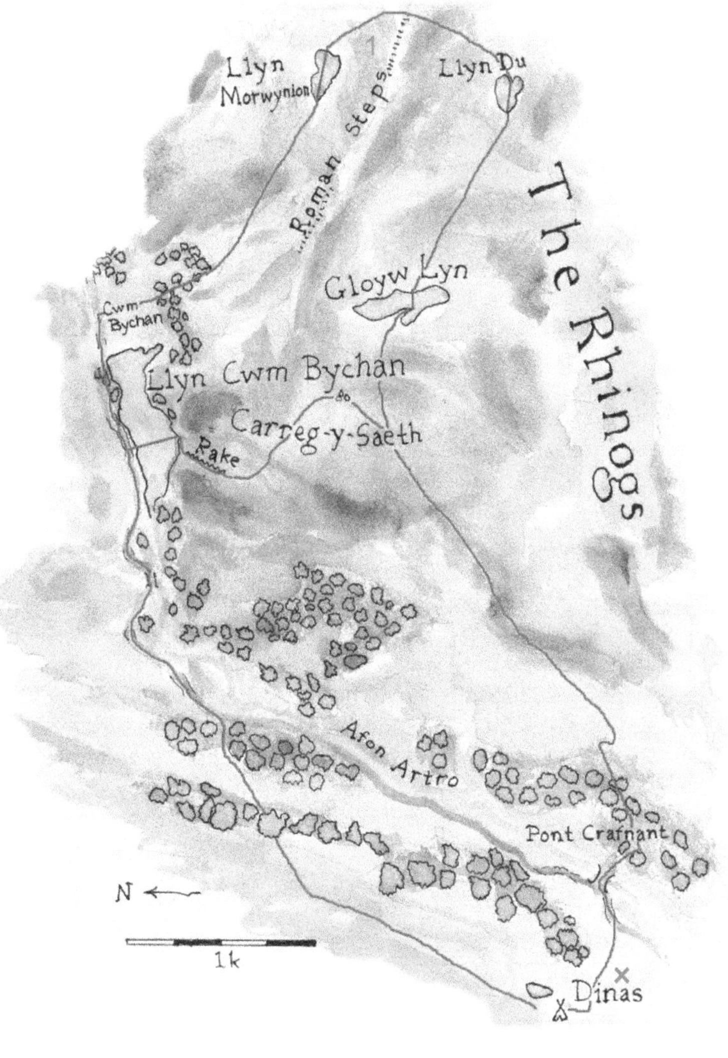

Llyn
Morwynion

Llyn Du

Roman Steps

Gloyw Lyn

Cwm
Bychan

Llyn Cwm Bychan

Carreg-y-Saeth

Rake

The Rhinogs

Afon Artro

Pont Crafnant

N ←

1 k

Dinas

18. Pembrokeshire

The coast of northern Pembrokeshire has dramatic cliffs but relatively few beaches. Once south of St David's Head, the countryside softens a bit; you walk past wild horses and a delicately balanced stone burial chamber and are soon amongst the surfers in the sweep of Whitesands Bay. Next door is the little beach below Pencarnan, where I spent childhood summer holidays. Heavenly in sunshine, when wet we would usually just sit in the tent playing scrabble and eating blackberries, but sometimes we would go to the nearby city (really a village) of St David's in the car. Here, nestling in the valley, is a most beautiful cathedral and the ruins of an ancient bishop's palace on the site of a yet older monastery. Between the cathedral and the palace flows the river Alun, with a ford, and it was the greatest treat of the holiday to drive through it.

David and his monks founded the monastery back in the sixth century, although their neighbours, Chief-Druid Bwya and his wife, disliked them and made various efforts to be rid of them. First, they simply attempted to massacre them all, but this was thwarted by God. Then they got their servant girls to bathe naked in the Alun to try and drive the holy men away. I am not quite sure how the Bwyas expected this ruse to work, but in any event, it failed; David and the monks stayed put. The remainder of this tale becomes increasingly unsavoury, so let us move on to Caerfai Bay, sandy and sheltered, where organised bands of wetsuited adventurers arrive to explore the coastal cliffs. Now follow the path east along the great sweep of St Brides Bay, past Solva, the white-trousered yachtsman's harbour, then south along the sands of windswept Newgale, narrow Nolton and horse-galloping Druidston to the twin beaches of Broad Haven and Little Haven, the home of some of my relatives and ancestors.[*]

---

[*] One of my ancestors at Little Haven donated the Green to the village. She was single and wealthy and we had great expectations of her. But then, when she died, all my parents got was an old cutlery set. We did not know quite what to do with it and so we put it in the back of the garage, and eventually gave it to a charity shop. Later we found out that it was actually quite valuable.

Broad Haven and Little Haven

At low tide you can walk along the sand between Broad Haven and Little Haven, at high tide, you can swim between them—either direction works equally well. Then you can buy yourself a snack and walk back over the cliff road.

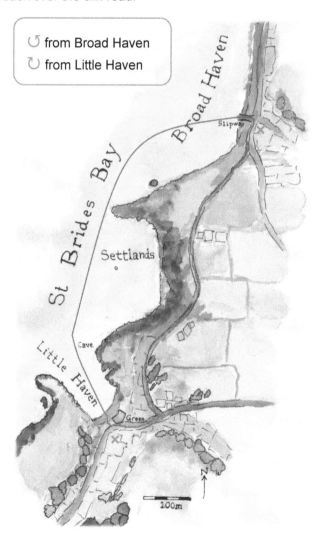

↺ from Broad Haven

↻ from Little Haven

This road between Broad Haven and Little Haven, is exceptionally steep and winding, and car drivers can avoid it by a short diversion. But most insist on using it anyway.

Weever fish.

Another hazard, at low tide, are weever fish; you may want to wear beach shoes. Those who tread on the poisonous spines of the fish say that they find it most unpleasant, though apparently urine helps.

This natural and obvious route between the two havens has long been a favourite of mine, but in the last few years, as swimhiking has gained in popularity, I have started coming across people in the water coming the other way. I should add that I take no credit for swimhiking taking off in Britain. My previous book never sold that many copies and I think it would have happened anyway as a natural variant of the wild swimming epidemic. But perhaps I should rather say that I do not accept any *blame* for the increasing number of people swimhiking, as I rather preferred it back in the good old days when I was almost invariably alone. It is not that I dislike bumping into other people in the middle of the sea or wherever, but the way that they so often swim on by, resolutely ignoring me. And so, between Little Haven and Broad Haven the usual pattern unfolds. I swim along one way and there, splashing purposefully along the other way—a fellow swimhiker! How serendipitous to converge on one another! So I tread water and stop for a chat.

"Hi there! Nice day! A bit wavy but … Oh." They keep their head down and swim on.

My father used to tell a story that began:

"It was a beautiful, sunny day, and Little Noddy was driving through the countryside to his friend Big Ears' house."

After a lovely ride, Little Noddy finally knocks on the door of the hollow tree where Big Ears lives. Big Ears opens the door.

"Hello Big Ears. It's Me. Little Noddy. I've come to play with you."
"Go away Noddy."

It makes me feel a bit like that.

Of course, the same thing can happen in the mountains; not every hiker responds to a cheery hello. Still, the proportion of people that behave like this in the water seems higher. Why is this? At first, I thought it was *them*, but now I think it is me: there must be something faintly off-putting about looking up to see my disembodied grinning face bobbing about in the waves. On land, a hiker can see not just my head but my whole body, and this reassures them that I am, in fact, just the right shape to stop and chat to: Rather than looking forbiddingly tough and fit, I am fat enough to look friendly and avuncular, but without being *so* fat as to appear morbidly obese. But in the water, people cannot really tell. So they assume the worse and swim on past.

From Little Haven the coastal path continues west to form the southern side of Saint Brides Bay. Below a twelfth century church, a small inlet, which rather confusingly is also called Saint Brides, has safe, sheltered swimming for children. The cliff path then turns south to Musselwick, where at low tide you can walk round to a sandy beach. But the beach is not accessible for long, the waves are soon back, and families must retreat before they are cut off as the rising tide begins to rush and crash amongst the grey black rocks. At one time you could dive in off these rocks with a swimsac, swim round to the beach and climb a steep, exposed and prickly path up the cliff. But the path has fallen into disuse, and the last time I tried it, I vowed that I never would again.

From Musselwick, we leave the coast to walk inland up the path to Marloes village, the starting point of our second swimhike.

Marloes

Rocks at Marloes Sands

Marloes Sands are magnificent, and even if you have never been there, you will undoubtedly have seen a photo of them. Despite its fame and beauty, the beach remains remarkably unspoiled by human beings, perhaps because you have to walk there. It has been a favourite spot for our family holidays since my childhood and it was here, last summer, that we said our final goodbyes to my mother, her younger grandchildren grabbing handfuls of her ashes and enthusiastically throwing them into the air from the cliff path.

The swimhike first takes you from the village to the beach. Rounding the final bend of the beach path, children hope to see sand to play on, but we swimhikers are hoping that the sea is high against the cliffs because although you can swim regardless of the state of the tide, the route is much more exciting if you *have to* swim to complete it. If the tide is indeed high, then providing the sea is reasonably calm, you can pick your way in past the boulders at the top of the main beach and swim east around rocky islands to the shingle beach on the other side of the cliff.

From the shingle, take the path up the cliff and join the coastal path east to the edge of the old aerodrome, which lies half way between Marloes and the next village of Dale. Its buildings are gone but the runways are still there: from the air, Nazca lines. One runway serves as a path. Join it when you reach a circle of concrete—I suppose a place for the planes to turn. From here, follow the footpath, farm road and bridleway back to the village.

To explore further, you might want to visit the tidal island of Gateholm. You might also want to visit Marloes Mere. It has a bird hide, and it is also a place of historic interest, as it was from this mere that doctors from all over the country obtained their leeches.*

Marloes Cricket

Marloes is famous, in our family, as the birthplace of Marloes Cricket. You need at least three players, a tennis ball, and a bat of some kind—a tennis racket is best. One person is the batsman, the others are bowlers and fielders. There are no teams; everyone plays for themselves. The purpose of the game, if you are one of the bowlers and fielders, is to become the batsman. If you are the batsman, your purpose is to continue as the batsman for as long as possible.

The game works as follows:

1. The bowler stands a few yards away from the batsman and throws him the ball in a gentle underarm bowl. Fielders stand wherever they please.

2. The batsman, who is holding the bat in front of him with both hands, deliberately hits the ball in the air so that at least one person, either the bowler or a fielder, can be reasonably expected to catch it before it bounces.

3. Whether or not the ball is caught, whoever grabs it first thereby becomes the bowler and throws another gentle bowl to the batsman, and so on.

4. If someone catches the ball twice in a row, (that is, on two successive good bowls without anyone else catching or dropping the ball in between them), then they become the batsman. As soon as there is a new batsman, the game starts afresh.

5. If there are three or more bowlers/fielders, then there are two ways of becoming the batsman: you can either (a) catch the ball twice in a row, or (b) be the first to catch the ball three times.

---

* Swimming in Marloes Mere is not recommended.

And that is about it. The game is particularly good for being *inclusive*. If, for example, you are useless at catching the ball because you are, say, only five years old this would, in most ball games, put you at a considerable disadvantage. However, in Marloes Cricket you will find that the batsman will direct the ball towards you again and again, giving you ample chance to catch it, even while he trusts that you will drop it

I have to admit that there are also difficulties with the game: people get over excited; they push each other; they stand directly in front of any five-year-olds playing, and so on. There are also endless disputes over: (a) what counts as a *bad bowl* that the batsman could not be reasonably expected to hit in the air so as to give a catch, and (b) what counts as a *bad hit* when no one could have been reasonably expected to catch the ball. If the batsman gives a bad hit, it is generally agreed that he should be out. But then who should replace him? The bowler? But that gives the bowler an incentive to throw a marginal bowl. My view is that the batsman should be replaced by anyone *but* the bowler. However, this too is a matter of dispute and these finer rules have never been definitively settled.

Marloes Village
Of Marloes it is said that that the whole community, fishermen and labourers, priest, farmers and all, were once wreckers: on stormy nights they would tie a lamp to the tail of a horse and set it a gallop along the edge of the cliff. But if this were ever true it certainly is no more, if for no other reason than that satellite navigation has made it obsolete. Now the village is notable for its handy shop, its clocktower and its church to St Peter the Fisherman. Inside the church is an old picture carved on wood of mermaids looking rather like seals. There is also a memorial to the members of 304 Squadron who died in the war.

Dale Aerodrome
The heroic men of No. 304 Polish Squadron suffered terrible losses as they fought the Nazi invasion of continental Europe from airbases in Britain. In the Spring of 1942, those who remained were transferred to Dale Aerodrome and were given the relatively safe job of patrolling the Atlantic for submarines. But it was not that safe.

On the morning of October 16 1942, Stanislaw Targowski received a letter from his wife back in Poland. It was the first time that he had heard from her since they were forced to part in 1939, and who can say what were his feelings of joy and relief as he read it. Later that morning he piloted a Wellington aircraft to search for submarines in the Bay of Biscay. Also on board were Gerard Twardoch, Tdeusz Oles, Zygmunt Piechowiak, Wladyslaw Mlynarski and Franciszek Kubacik. After they had taken off, a telegram arrived at the aerodrome to say that F/O Targowski had been awarded the Distinguished Flying Cross. The rest of the squadron prepared an impromptu party to celebrate the good news when the crew returned.

In the air, two German fighter pilots spotted the plane. Targowski tried to escape but they caught him up and one of them shot him with a machine gun. He slumped over the controls and the Wellington crashed into the sea. The Germans must have circled, because they reported seeing a yellow dinghy, which suggests that at least some of the crew yet survived. At this point the German narrative stops. There were no survivors.

Church Rock

Below Milford Haven, I am less familiar with the coast, but know that Broad Haven South is a marvellous place. The beach is wide and fringed with dunes. Children can squeeze through a cave: in at one end and out the other. Adults can saunter round the lily ponds. There is a dramatic cliff path, a great hole to edge around. And there is Church Rock.

We are a large family party and after plonking our stuff down at base camp at the top of the beach, some sit down while others wander off to explore. And there out to sea, but not very far out to sea, is Church Rock. Over the roar of the waves I hear it ask me a question:

"Why don't you swim round me?"

I look at the water. The sea is a bit rough and the waves are approaching the beach at a 45 degree angle. The tide, though, appears to be low meaning both slack water, and less distance, although the loop is a bit further than it appears because of the need to keep wide of the rock

"Why don't you swim round me, *coward*?"

"All right, I will."

Swimming around an island or some other feature is not a swimhike as you come out at more or less the same place that you came in, but it *feels* like a swimhike because it is purposeful, you have a definite objective to achieve and a natural route to follow. In this case, before Church Rock itself there are two smaller rocks and I set out to circle all three, keeping a good gap to ensure I am not swept onto them.

Church Rock

At first everything goes as planned. I swallow a mouthful of water, but this just alerts me to be more careful. I pass the first and smallest rock. I pass the second mid-sized rock. I draw level with the main rock with its spire. Waves roll in and water tosses as other waves are flung back by the rock or force their way past with leaping spray. I continue to swim out to sea in a wide circle, keeping my distance until it is time to turn. Now I swim in the direction of the waves. I draw abreast of Church Rock and am swept by quickly and easily. A few strokes more and I am in the lee of the rock and shielded from the waves. It is time to get back to shore.

I leave the protection of the big rock and swim until I am sheltered by the mid-sized rock, then swim on. The going is now much slower as I counter the push of the current, but eventually I close the gap to reach the third smaller rock. This rock lies opposite the jutting rocky point that is the eastern lip of the bay. Beneath the point there is white water as the waves crash against the cliffs, so I need to swim into the current a short way in order to come out on the beach. And: Oh look! Tiny figures. There are people watching me, at a distance, on the sand. They are too small to make out, but perhaps they are my relatives. Well, whoever they are, I am on to the easy bit now. I will swim along between the third rock and the shore until I draw level with the sand. And then I won't get out straight away but carry on further into the current, doing butterfly, to give my audience a bit of a show.

I turn on my back to swim into the current. Behind me, as far as I can see, the cliffs stretch, apparently unbroken, to a distant peninsula. The strength of the cross current starts to dawn on me. The straight-line distance between the third rock and the beach is not very great, but I am not getting any closer. My problem is that the cross current is strong and unless I swim more or less directly into it, I am pushed away from the beach to the line of cliffs. I swim and I swim, and I get nowhere. I pause for a moment and straight away I am pushed back. By now I realise how strongly the sea is flowing though the gap between the third rock and the shore and a strange mental adjustment occurs as I undergo a rapid transition from planning to show off to the people on the beach to realising that *I may drown.*

The idea that one-day-I-will-die is usually is just a string of words that means nothing to me. Now, all of a sudden, it *does* mean something, something very immediate, something that I can anticipate happening... Where?—I look back into the middle distance of the wave tossed sea—in an hour or two, just around *there.* For some reason, I am envisaging drowning not from my own perspective but rather from that of the people on the beach. They would be helpless, anxious if relatives, watching me battling vainly against the current, being swept away and eventually vanishing from view. How long did I have? I was avoiding using the word 'rip tide' to myself, but I knew it well enough and knew that people caught in a rip tide drowned from exhaustion. But then what option did I have but to fight the current? As I saw it in the water, I *had* to reach the beach or be swept back past endless cliffs. There *might* be a place to land further down, but I could not see one. I remembered the stories of channel swimmers who were close, very close, to Cap Gris Nez, and then the tide changed and they could not swim the final yards, no matter how they tried. I felt like that, so close to the shore yet unable to reach it, the people watching unable to help.

I keep swimming. By now I am a bit nearer to the shore albeit by the rocks where landing is impossible. But perhaps, if I just keep swimming backcrawl, I will make it; my pectoral muscles are tired, but I know I can yet swim on my back for a long time. So I swim and I swim and I swim. As I swim, there is another mental transition; I start to realise that I *am*, very gradually, making progress and that, as long as I *keep* making progress, I will *not* be swept away and will not drown after all. So, when my foot finally touches down, this is no great moment. It is back to what I expected. Except that I had expected to be farther along beach, after doing a bit of butterfly.

I wade out of the waves onto the very far end of the beach. No one is there to greet me. The watchers all seem to have disappeared. Were they ever watching me at all? I walk back along the sand, then run. At base camp my sister Alison and her husband Greg are lying on tatami mats. My son Nicholas and his cousin Oliver are exploring the mouth of the cave. The others are off on the beach playing Marloes Cricket.

Mistakes

1. *Insufficient account of rough water.* When the water is rough currents are stronger, and all the buffeting tires you more quickly.

2. *Insufficient account of a plainly visible cross current.* Oops.

3. *Not knowing the state of the tide.* I guessed it was low tide, but was wrong; the tide continued to go out for a couple of hours.

4. *Not finding out about the coastline in the vicinity of the swim.* Had I done a recce, or even looked at a map, I would have been much better informed about my options if caught in a current. In particular, I would have known that despite the appearance of endless cliffs there were, in fact, other beaches, including one just round the corner, so I could have relaxed, gone with the flow and got out further down.

All these things should be ascertained before attempting a route — or deciding that it is better not to. Once caught in a current in circumstances similar to Church Rock, the best choice is harder to gauge.

A. It may be that that *swimming close to the cliff gives shelter from the current.* If so, one could swim straight towards the shore without worrying about being pushed the wrong way and only then turn into the current to try and reach a safe landing place. But in rough weather, swimming in close brings its own risks of getting caught by breaking waves.

B. Conversely, it might be possible to escape a current by *swimming out to sea.* You could then reposition yourself to take account of the current before swimming back in. But as well as being psychologically daunting to swim out to sea to reach land, there is the unknown of how far might you have to go before the current weakens.

C. It might be best to concentrate on *conserving strength,* swimming merely to stay afloat while looking for whatever chances might arise. However, while this may save you from quickly becoming exhausted, there is cold to contend with, particularly when swimming without a wetsuit.

D. If people are watching, it might be best to *wave* at them to show you want help. (But I felt too proud to do that.)

CROSSING THE CHANNEL

Patriotic Englishmen like me have been brought up on the stories of the heroes of our past: Sir Francis Drake, Captain Scott, Captain Oates, and the first man to swim the channel, Captain Matthew Webb of Shropshire, on 24th August 1875. In fact, Paul Boyton had performed this feat in his rubber suit some three months earlier, but it has generally been decided that this did not count. Since that time, many determined and accomplished swimmers have made the crossing accompanied by boats. However, something else is also going on in the channel. As I, a citizen of a wealthy democracy, add a little thrill to my life while holidaying by getting caught in a current, undocumented migrants are adventuring in earnest. Prevented by carrier liability rules from simply catching a plane, train, boat or bus across international borders, they make their way, who knows how, to the coast of northern France and look for their chance to cross. I barely notice their existence, and was not thinking of them at all when, in *Swimhiking the Lake District and North East England*, I offered, rather lightly, to give a certificate to anyone who succeeded in swimhiking across the English Channel *without* an accompanying boat. Back then I thought that this would never happen. Now, with up to a thousand people a day venturing out in rubber dinghies, I fear that it is almost inevitable that someone will try. And although they will probably drown, they will possibly make it. Indeed, it appears that in August 2021 Mr Vaas Feniks Nokard, seeking asylum in Japan, accomplished a similarly arduous crossing from the Russian controlled island of Kunashiri to Shibetsu in Hokkaido.

With swimhiking the channel ruled out as far too dangerous, how are we to get to Europe (or to Britain if on the continent)? I personally have almost always flown. It is quick, cheap, and very convenient, with some airports, like those at Cavtat and Nice, so close to the beach that you can virtually start swimhiking from the terminal. On one occasion however, I did not fly but cycled to Newcastle and took the ferry to Holland to camp. This journey felt wholly different than taking a plane, as I sensed the ground beneath the wheels of my bike and the water beneath the rocking boat the whole way. Once there, swimhiking felt different too, it was not a

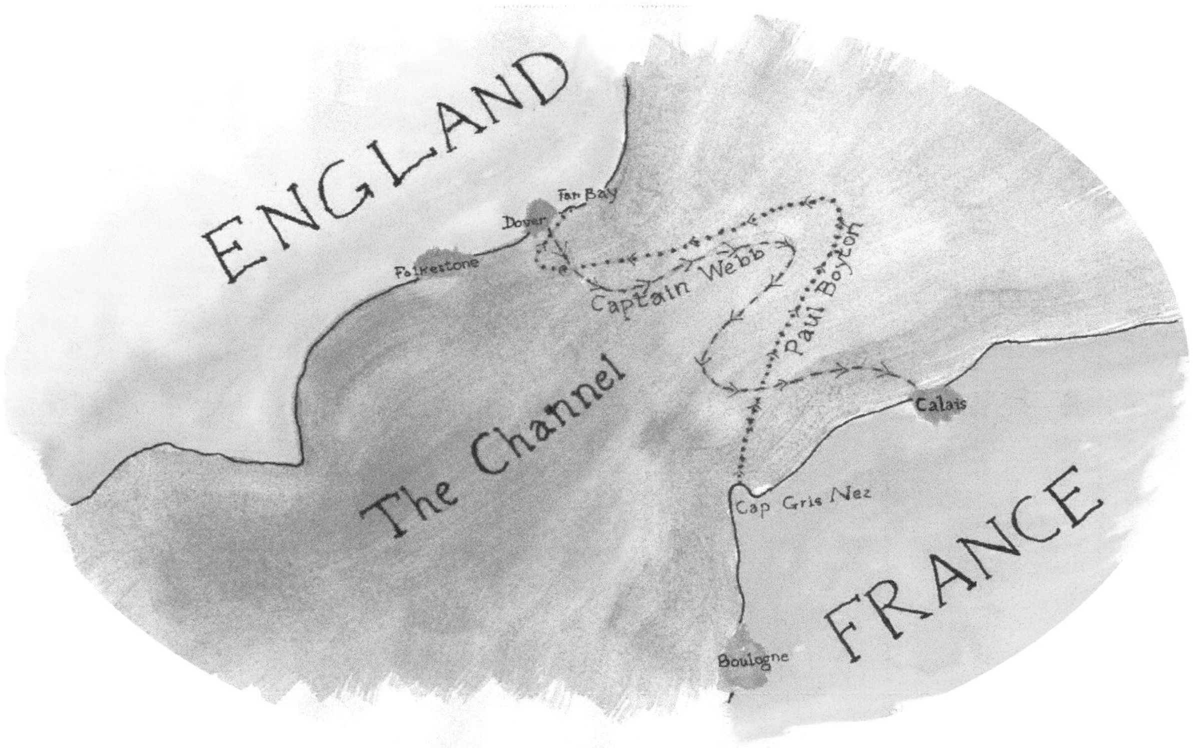

ENGLAND

The Channel

Folkestone

Dover

Fan Bay

Captain Webb

Paul Boyton

Boulogne

Cap Gris Nez

Calais

FRANCE

self-contained little loop, but was as one with the whole trip. Holland, admittedly, is not very far away from Britain, but my nephew Daniel has cycled all the way back from Croatia. So I encourage *you* to travel overland, preferably by horse or by bicycle, and by boat or train. We are not built to fly in the air. We can jump up and down and ballet dancers seem to float for a fraction of a second, but this aside, the closest we can get to flying through the air by our own unaided efforts is falling through it as we leap or dive from the land into the water. It may be better for ourselves, as well as the planet, to leave it at that.*

Just as a rucksack can be turned into a swimsac, so surely can a bicycle be somehow turned into a pedalo...

---

* Jumping and diving into the water also has strict natural limits. In 1885, Robert Odlum argued otherwise, reasoning that air is perfectly safe to fall through, and water safe to land in. Encouraged by his friend Paul Boyton, who was taking bets on the outcome from a boat beneath, Odlum tested his theory by jumping from Brooklyn Bridge. Unfortunately, he died; his argument might have appeared sound, but when it comes to hitting water after accelerating from a great height, it is not. Lesser heights also carry dangers. A mother on a bus showed me photos of her son, in a wheelchair; he had dived off a pier when he was sixteen and broken his neck. Nonetheless, people, and young men especially, jump from cliffs the whole time. Swimhikers need to be aware of this, particularly in the Mediterranean where being hit from above by a young man is one more hazard to deal with, along with sea urchins, jellyfish and jet skiers.

Part Two

EUROPE

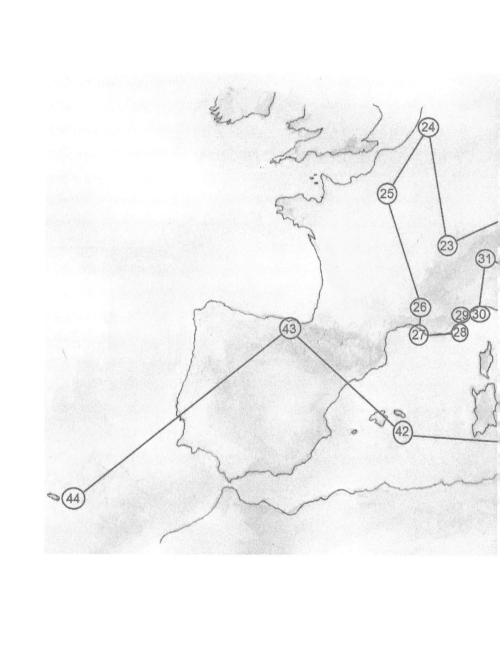

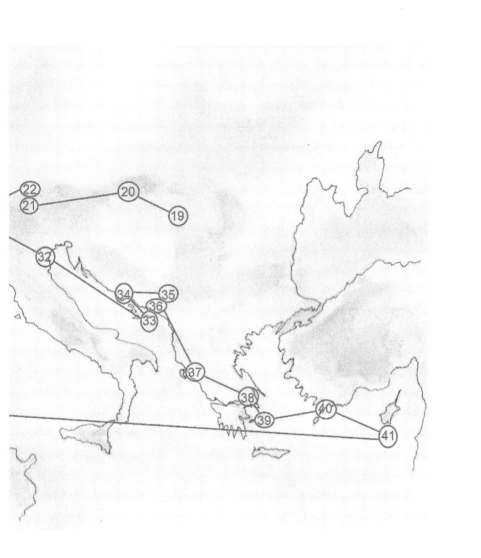

Hungary

19. Budapest

Where better to begin our tour of the continent than in Hungary's capital Budapest. It has many fine sights. It has monuments to its turbulent and often tragic history. It has several ornate, indoor thermal pools where one can sit and luxuriate, and some outdoor ones too. It has a superb McDonald's restaurant.

"Yes, yes, yes," I hear you say. "But where might one actually *swimhike*?"

This question is a little trickier. The Danube is the obvious place, as it does not flow all that fast through Budapest, but it still looks rather daunting. Perhaps Lake Balaton, to the west? This long narrow lake has an organised crossing each year, with boats transporting the swimmers' belongings, which suggests it might be excellent swimhiking country. Maybe in some places it is, but all I know is that on the southern shore, at Sifiok, you have to pay to use the beach and the water is endlessly shallow. I never got much above my knees, and I am not sure that you are even allowed to, as there was some rule about not venturing more than 500m from the shore. To the north of the country at Esztergom, things are more promising. Protected by a gravel bank, the Danube above the bridge at this historic town is safe for family swimming. Below the bridge, the river wends its way down between green mountains, and past castles and beaches before bending into Budapest, and for much of the way it looks ideal for swimhiking, particularly the first section to Visegrad. I cannot say *for sure* whether it is because we took the ferry, although Paul Boyton certainly seems to have enjoyed it. Higher up the river, near Komorn, Boyton had dropped asleep as he floated down the Danube in his rubber suit and awoke to find himself being bashed around the head by a mill paddle suspended between two barges. However, after recuperating on shore he returned to the water, and at Visegrad fell in with a rowing boat, whose occupants included "the most lovely girl he had ever seen." They talk; they share a glass of wine; she unpins a bunch of violets from her breast and passes them to him. After gallantly kissing them, Boyton stuffs them into his rubber suit before floating on down to Budapest. Here he is greeted by vast crowds shouting 'Long live Boyton! Long Live America!' Later, the same girl reappears, accompanied by a savagely jealous army officer. But enough about Boyton: we need to get back to Budapest and find somewhere there to go swimhiking.

In the middle of the Danube in Budapest lies Margaret Island. The island has a stony shoreline that makes it relatively easy to get in and out of the water and there is plenty to see, including the grave where Saint Margaret lies buried; an elegant spa hotel; a large fenced open air thermal pool and swimming bath complex; landscaped grounds including a Japanese garden, and a children's zoo. There is also a well-used bouncy jogging track around the island's perimeter, along which everyone runs anti-clockwise. This swimhike follows the flow of the joggers round the bouncy path but also pops in and out of the Danube, in a cautious kind of way, on the northwest shore of the island. Do not be too cautious however, as if you swim too close to the shore you will bump your knees on the rocks.

Once you have got out the great river unscathed, you can relax in two rocky hot pools. These pools are built right on the bank and are very comfortable, with great views. They are not advertised but are open to anyone to find and to use, although the few people that *do* use them seem mostly to be vagrants.

Saint Margaret, you can be sure, would have been sympathetic to these down and outs. When she lived in a convent on the island in the thirteenth century, she spent her time tending the sick wearing dirty old clothes, resolutely maintaining her single life of service in the face of parental efforts to arrange a dynastic marriage. If the chroniclers are to be believed (I don't), she also secretly engaged in what sound like sado-masochistic practices to show how holy she was. Margaret has been firmly thought of as a saint in Hungary ever since, to the extent that Hungarians are perplexed as to why it took the Pope until 1943 to confirm that indeed she was one. From an outsider's perspective, however, some doubt remains; there is

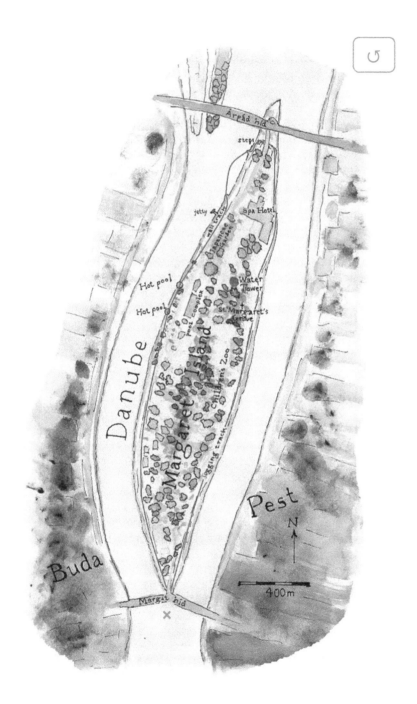

certainly much evidence that Margaret was kind and good, but her only miracles seem to have been rescuing a pot of crayfish from the fire without getting her hands burnt, and smelling of roses after she died.

Ignaz Semmelweis also cared for the sick. He is commemorated in Budapest by a statue, and by a museum in the house where he was born, one containing antiquated medical implements. As a doctor running two maternity wards in Vienna in the 1840s, Semmelweis noticed that far more women were dying in the ward attended by medical students than were dying in the ward attended by midwives. Semmelweis gave the matter much thought, made various experimental changes to the student ward, and eventually worked out why the death rates were so different: unlike the midwives, the students dissected cadavers as part of their training, and then went on to examine women and deliver babies with dirty hands, infecting their patients with a form of blood poisoning.

As soon as he realised what was happening, Semmelweis instituted a strict hand washing regimen and the death rate in the medical student ward in Vienna went right down. The problem was solved. Eagerly he told all his colleagues about it and wrote to the medical journals. But few took much notice, and even those who did pretended that they would have washed their hands *anyway* and didn't need *him* to tell them that, and when Semmelweis started to make a fuss about it and suggest—perhaps not very diplomatically—that by ignoring his discovery his colleagues were killing the women in their care, he lost his job. Eventually, Semmelweis went mad. He was confined to a mental home, and when he tried to escape, he was beaten to death.

Now Semmelweis is extolled for making a great medical advance, and of course he did, although his method of working things out by trial and error was not new. What *was* new, however, was the development of a medical *profession* with the power, when it suited it, to suppress the truth. After hundreds of years in which reasoning people had patiently argued against the obdurate irrationality with which religions attempted to enforce compliance with *their* supposed truths, the Semmelweis affair was the first sign that the emerging medical-scientific complex was going to adopt exactly the same dogmatic approach.

Austria

20. Vienna

To go swimhiking in Vienna you first need to head for the beautiful blue Danube. The Vorgartenstrasse underground station is close by and look! There it is! We peer down at a very large, dirty brown, fast flowing river, full of barges and tour boats.

Eeugh! We are certainly not going to go swimhiking in *there*. No, let us continue straight across the Danube on a bridge. Almost immediately we arrive at the Neue Donau or New Danube which, although it is separated from the Danube by only one or two hundred yards, is *completely* different. The New Danube, in fact, is swimhike heaven, with flocks of swans to accompany us in the place of angels.

Having escorted you to the New Danube, there is really very little else for me to do. The water is clear and blue and even tastes quite nice. There are no motorised boats. There is parkland all along the banks. You can get in and out at almost any point; you can swim across from one side to another; you can swim down river for miles. You can even swim *up* river for miles as the current is very slight.

Even heaven gets tiresome eventually, however, and when it does, you may wish to explore two further lakes nearby, or rather one large oxbow lake divided into two: the Ober Alte Donau, or Upper Old Danube and the Untere Alte Donau, or Lower Old Danube. The Upper Old Danube is reedy but still makes for a pleasant excursion and can be combined with the New Danube in a satisfying swimhike. The Lower Old Danube is surrounded by minutely parcelled and jealously guarded private property. If you try to go swimhiking there you will fall from heaven very sharply back to earth.

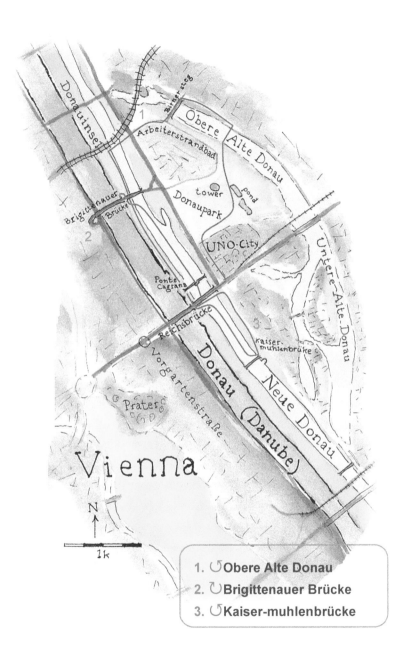

Vienna

N

1k

1. ↺Obere Alte Donau
2. ↻Brigittenauer Brücke
3. ↺Kaiser-muhlenbrücke

In between the New and Old Danube is 'UNO City', huge and modern and—until we have global government—of somewhat uncertain purpose (aside from making a great backdrop for superhero and monster movies), with not much to see. However, in the centre of Vienna there are, of course, many fantastic cultural sites that are open daily.

What is there to do on a summer's evening? After buying expensive tickets to listen to Mozart being played by musicians in wigs, we discovered what *Austrians* do at night: visit the Prater Amusement Park. The fairground rides are spectacular. Muscular men hit a boxing ball incredibly hard. And with a blithe disregard for Health and Safety, there are furious five minute motor races around a tiny track, where anyone can join in. A man starts right at the back, skilfully weaves his way through; yells at someone to get out of his way; smashes past them. Now it is the final lap. A girl has done remarkably well, but the man is ruthless. Crash! He rams her into the side and races to the line. Her car has stopped; she has to walk to the finish.

21. Seefeld

Before I had even set off on this swimhike, I had designated it as a timeless classic, a really satisfying natural loop around Brunschkopf from the small Tyrolean town of Seefeld, crossing three lakes along the way. So off I go, to the first lake, Wildmoossee. On the map it is a reasonably sized expanse of water a good five hundred yards long, but when I get there, the lake has gone. There is just a meadow, with a puddle in the middle of it. I must have gone wrong. I don't know how because visibility is perfect, but I *must* be somewhere else. I look carefully at the map. What is that written in parentheses underneath the lake? "Periodisch". Ah.

I continue on to Lottensee. This lake is also marked as periodic and when I get there, it too has drained away for the summer. Here there is not even a puddle.

Möserer See, *is* still there; it is a gorgeous little lake with an island, and is wonderful to swim in. But the lake really is not very big, and in the summer sun you will not so much want to swimhike across it as to simply laze about there with everyone else; the lake is very popular with families on a day out. I should add that Möserer See is surrounded by 'No Swimming' signs. However, in an interesting reversal of the situation that so often pertains in Britain, these are no swimming signs *for dogs*.

Back at Seefeld, I try swimhiking across Wildsee Bad on the southern edge of the town. There is a firm entry underfoot until you are about three foot deep, at which point the lake floor changes to a flat green mud. The level of the mud never varies so it *is* possible to swim across, even if your knees may bump into the mud now and again, but it is not especially nice. All in all, Seefeld, which is ringed by mountains and has excellent paths, is an ideal spot for hiking, but as far as swimhiking in the summer goes, it is not.

Germany

22. Mittenwald

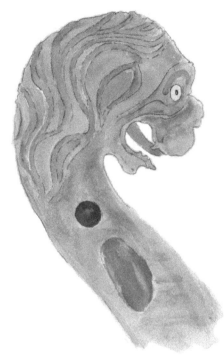

A track that follows the Laine river, up from Mittenwald in the German Alps, leads to Lautersee. The lake is clean with lots of little fish; it has beautiful views; it has grassy banks for sunbathing, and it is great for family swimhiking, with a lakeshore path that enables you to swim from one side to another in a number of ways.

Mittenwald has long been a centre for violin making in a tradition that lives on with several active workshops. A museum recreates a luther's studio and shows numerous locally made violins from down the centuries. It might be objected that this display is largely redundant as one violin tends to look very much like another. However, in the nineteenth century some of the luthers of Mittenwald introduced a bit of variety by carving the end of the instrument to look like a lion's head rather than a scroll. Sometimes they also added a bit of felt for its tongue.

The town is also a holiday makers destination; there are several hotels and regular trains from Munich. The station is bedecked with flowers, there are parks, there is tourist information. It is almost impossible to imagine that this industrious and pretty little place was a scene of horror in 1945 as the Nazis—conscious to the last of their image—started to empty Dachau concentration camp near Munich, sending starving inmates south toward Austria in death marches, or on a train that was then turned back at Seefeld on the other side of the border. Quite what happened to the prisoners who ended up in Mittenwald is unclear. By some accounts an unnamed local woman's appeal saved hundreds from being massacred. However, in 1946 it was also reported that "the graves of the Jews in the Mittenwald cemetery, who were murdered by the SS in the spring of 1945, will soon be rebuilt in dignified form."

Hannah Arendt, the theorist of totalitarianism, asks of terrible events of this type: 'How *could it* have happened?' Perhaps some small part of the answer is that most of us can be pushed gently towards genocide by a series of baby steps, with only a courageous few standing firm. Eight years earlier, in 1937, the Mittenwald Tourist Office was writing to the authorities in Munich: the signs by the rail line saying 'Jews are not wanted in Mittenwald' that had been taken down for the Olympics, yes, they could confirm that they would be putting them up again. They could confirm too that when Jews rented a place, it was usually enough to have a quiet word with the owners to recall them to their 'civic duty' (*staatsbürgerlichen Pflichten*). There was, in fact, only one exception: the Alpenhotel proprietor Erhard Erdt. In defiance of all instruction, Mr Erdt continued to allow Jewish guests. Not only that, but he was notorious for treating them courteously. A number of Aryan guests had complained about these things, and Erdt had then excluded *them* from his hotel. All this had been recorded in writing and forwarded to both the Nazi Party and the business association. Heil Hitler.*

---

* I know no more about Erhard Erdt. However, his business must have survived his defiance of the Nazis because after the war, at a time of tension between Jews and Ukrainians in Mittenwald's Displaced Persons Camp, Alpenhotel Erdt is made available for German Jews. Later the hotel became a retirement home, before being demolished.

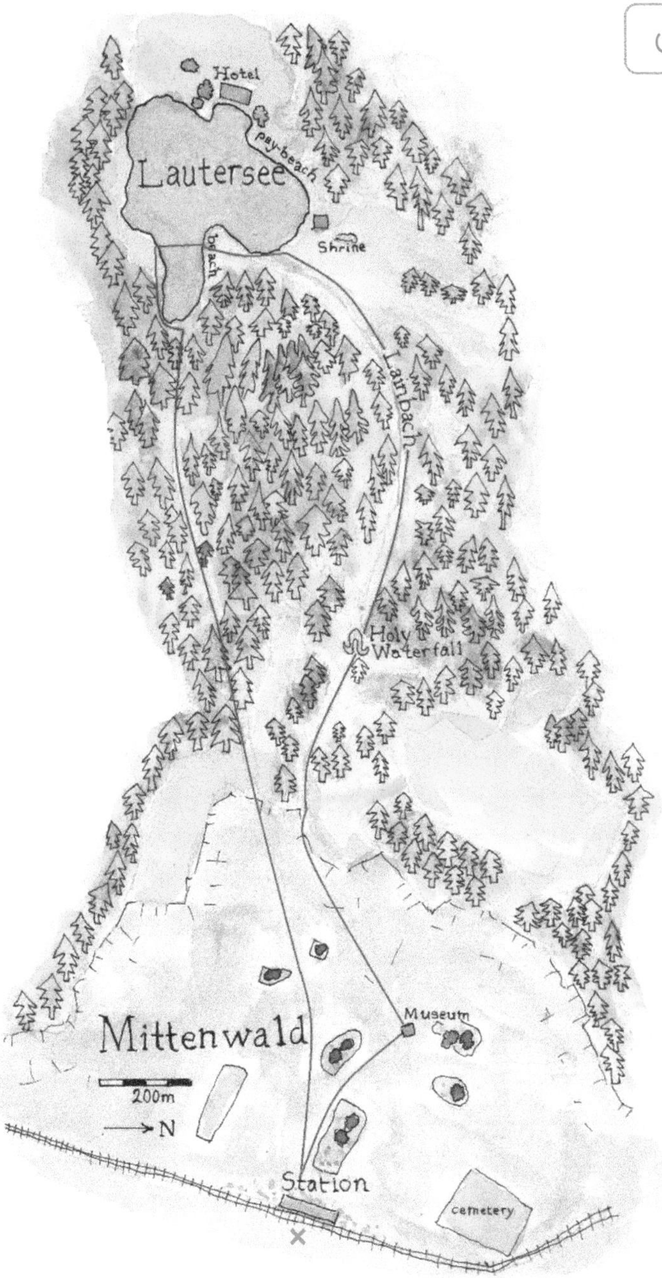
Hotel
pay-beach
Lautersee
beach
Shrine
Lainbach
Holy
Waterfall
Museum
Mittenwald
200m
N
Station
cemetery

Switzerland

23. Geneva

The centre of Geneva is full of 'no swimming' notices. Possibly the signs are there because people have tried to emulate Basel, where swimhiking down the Rhine has become an institution. Still, this is a rare case where the signs may provide good advice: in the fast flowing Rhone, swimming would be imprudent, as you would not so much swim as be swept off. Lake Leman, however, is placid, and in summer it is warm and just the place for a shoreline swimhike from Geneva's botanical gardens.

These gardens lie just below the grounds of the Palais des Nations, the old headquarters of the League of Nations, now used by the UN. We enter its great meeting room, where our guide tells us that countries are sat according to the alphabet.

"What is the first country to be seated, alphabetically?" he asks.
"Albania?" someone guesses.
"That is the second."
"Hmm..." I think to myself. "So, it obviously begins with an A, not Australia, not Austria, let me see..."
"Aberbaijan!" I shout out confidently. I am a politics lecturer after all.
"Azerbaijan is on the front row, certainly." the guide responds diplomatically.

I still do not know which country comes first. I have been too proud to look it up.

On a jetty at the end of the lake, the Jet d'eau shoots a fountain high into the air. You can, if you like, walk along beneath it, to within about eight feet of the spout. There is no safety rail along the jetty, no warning signs and indeed no health and safety apparatus at all, just people enjoying it. How would this be handled in Britain? 'Closed until Further Notice', says Toshie.

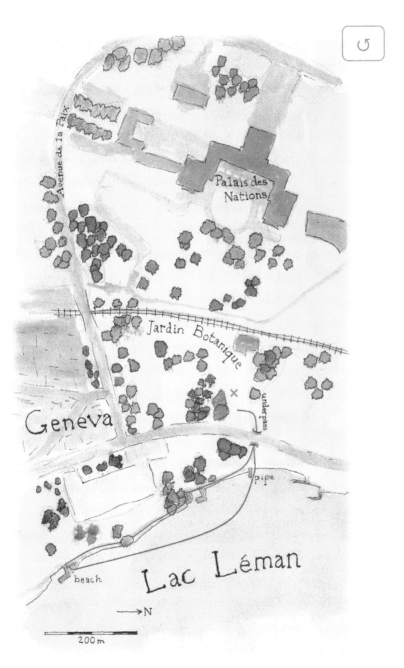

Holland

The Dutch are unusually welcoming to foreigners, going out of their way to make people feel at home. Almost as soon as I wheel my bicycle off the ferry at Ijmuiden I am accosted by helpful fellow cyclists, and this hospitality continues throughout my visit. This would give reason enough to visit Holland even if the only swimhiking opportunities were shoreline routes along its pleasant sand duned coast. But it is inland that the best adventures lie. Here the water network that the Dutch have created is so enticing that it hard not to view it as one that has been made specifically for the enjoyment of swimhikers, with land reclamation and the drainage and irrigation of fields and things like that, mere minor subsidiary benefits.

24. Rijpwetering

The Kagerplassen area, outside Leiden, is a near-ideal. There are manmade lakes, islands, canals, windmills, everything you could possibly wish for, and all would be perfect were it not for two other manmade features of the area. The first are property rights along the waterside, with much 'verboten' signage, although as we swimhikers do not leave our clothes a hostage to fortune on the shore, we need not worry about this too much. However, swimhikers are as vulnerable as any other swimmers to the second problem: the speed at which some of the boats are driven.

From Rijpwetering, a short swimhike takes you through two lakes, Koppoel and Kleipoel, as well as past three windmills. A road from the village, leads to the Koeppel Windmill. Part way along is a low bridge over a small lily filled canal, and a convenient grassy entry point for Koppoel. Swim past the windmill for the wide River Waterloos. The river bends into Kleipoel, where you can head for Lijkermolen 1 Windmill, exiting at the little beach nearby. Take the road back to Rijpwetering, pausing along the way to admire Lijkermolen 2 Windmill. With thatched roofs and domestic gardens

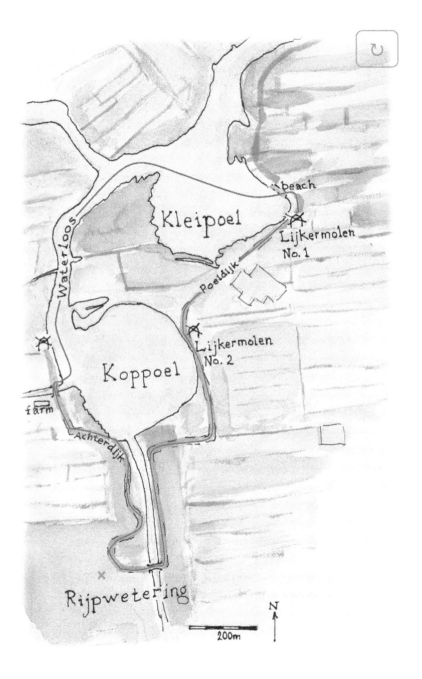

beach

Kleipoel

Lijkermolen No. 1

Waterloos

Poeldijk

Lijkermolen No. 2

Koppoel

farm

Achterdijk

×

Rijpwetering

N

200m

beneath the sails, these windmills look most picturesque and, like all windmills, no doubt they are fascinating within.

At the campsite, seeing that I am alone, a pleasant Dutch family befriends me. I join in their games. I teach them Marloes Cricket. We chat. The father explains how he dresses up at the weekend to stage World War Two reenactments. He shows me photographs. They invite Germans to come over and join in with them too: there was (vaguely) some problem about them doing it in Germany.

France

25. Paris

Bassin de la Villette

In comparison to the nearby canals, and indeed the Seine, the water in the Bassin de la Villette, a large oblong artificial lake, appears fairly salubrious. The Bassin was completed in 1808 and when, in 1832, there was a cholera outbreak in Paris, the relative cleanliness of the water may help to explain why mortality rates in the area were slightly better than in the worst affected places around the Île de la Cité. Not all of the deaths were caused by cholera. A fearful, virtuous, and infuriated crowd beat several entirely innocent people to death for supposedly spreading the disease. Thank goodness that now, with covid being blamed on the unvaccinated, things are much more civilised, with President Macron merely wanting to "emmerder" or shit on them. What a wise and statesmanlike policy. In the fullness of time, the great man will doubtless have many statues erected in his honour, many splendid boulevards named after him.

The Bassin is a nice spot for a swimhike. It is even legal, more or less, as after the persistent flouting of the no swimming rules and a number of 'spontaneous events', swimming has now been officially allowed there, albeit in a confined and regulated manner. Possibly, even those who are not fully vaccinated may be allowed to into the water, although I am not quite sure of this, as in January 2022 they were banned from outdoor swimming pools.

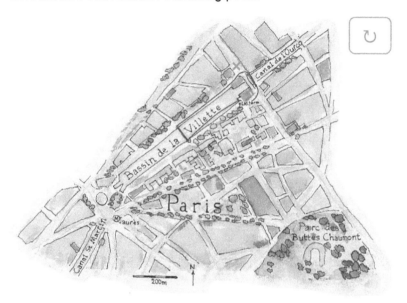

Around the banks of the Bassin is a cheerful scene of restaurants (for the vaccinated only), boules games and public houseboats, so you may feel that there is little reason to stray further. However, for those wishing for a more ambitious hike than the one shown on the map, there are three options:

(1) Follow the Canal de l'Ourcq (which is soupy, so I recommend going on foot) to La Villette, with its science and music museums.

(2) Explore the pleasantly hilly Parc des Buttes-Chaumont and if you wish—though there is nothing particular to see—continue on to visit Place Hannah Arendt. How nice to have a square in Paris named after you, even a small and obscure one! I like to imagine that after I am dead, Parisians will designate somewhere as Place

Peter Hayes. (The only thing that spoils this daydream is that I cannot think of the slightest reason why they should.)

(3) Follow the Canal St Martin (which disappears into a tunnel, so I definitely recommend going on foot) to the Place Bastille. The storming of the Bastille in 1789 was the starting point of the French Revolution. The Bastille, though, is no longer there, as after storming it, the revolutionaries knocked it down. They also cut off the governor's head, which seems rather hard as he did his best to be reasonable, including inviting them in for breakfast. In paintings of the great event, the Bastille is depicted as a huge imposing building. However, it has been suggested that this is just to make the revolutionaries look braver than they really were and that the fort was actually rather small.

From the Place Bastille it is an easy walk into central Paris, which is full of wonderful sights. However, the site of what was once the most famous of them all has virtually nothing to commemorate it. When you get to the Place de la Révolution, now renamed Place de la Concorde, you have to negotiate the traffic to get to the middle, where all there is to see is a small brass plaque where the thing once stood. And that is it. Every street vendor sells miniature Eiffel Towers and often has copies of the Arc de Triomphe and the Sacre Coeur as well, but where are all the little guillotines?

The French Revolution is still a hotly debated event. The republican intellectuals have the upper hand in promulgating their views on the topic as *they* curate the museums. Nonetheless, theirs is not the only perspective. An alternative view, popular amongst Catholics, is that the revolution was fundamentally evil, and its victims, martyrs and saints. In particular, sainthood is attributed to Queen Marie Antoinette, guillotined in 1793. The Vatican has not taken up the calls for her canonisation, perhaps because some aspects of her life were not beyond reproach, but the campaign continues. The latest effort has been to establish her sainthood by proxy by calling for Marie Antionette's sister-in-law Elisabeth, guillotined in 1794, to be canonised. In his official letter on the matter, in 2017, the Archbishop of Paris explained how Elisabeth had comforted those with her in the cart to the scaffold and even managed to save one, the Comtesse de Sérilly, by persuading her to reveal that she was pregnant. Then, at the moment when Elisabeth was beheaded, the scent of roses wafted over the onlookers in the square.

The Conciergerie, where both Marie Antionette and Elisabeth were imprisoned, is mainly given over to revolutionary propaganda. Yes, there were one or two difficulties or unfortunate occurrences during the revolution, but there were *many* marvellous achievements that were the result of its extraordinary humanitarian progressiveness etc etc. Reading these things, one is led to the chapel to Marie Antionette, built in 1816 at the time of the Restoration. But is it a shrine or merely a place where the traitor (for that is what she was) may once have been? It is a contested space, the meeting point of the Catholic veneration of her relics (her shift, a piece of her belt, a lock of her hair) and the republican contempt for those who would oppose the rights of man.

This discussion may be felt to be a little austere. There is a swimhiking route, there is a bit of history, but seeing as (a) the chapter is, after all, about *Paris* and that (b) this book—ostensibly at least—is a sort of *guidebook*, then surely (c) there should be some kind of restaurant recommendation? As a matter of fact, I do know of an excellent restaurant in Paris: highly atmospheric with wood-lined walls, high fanned ceilings, cheap tasty food, excellent house wine and waiters that scrawl the bill on the paper tablecloth. However, the last time I went there, I noticed that as the waiter collected up the plates left behind by his last set of customers, he deposited their uneaten chips on to the plate being prepared for one of his next set of customers. He then presented this plate with an elaborate and courtly flourish, much to the delight of the lady who had ordered it.

I said nothing. It would do her no harm, it would help to save the planet, and all in all it seemed better to keep quiet. Even so, I feel that I cannot now recommend this restaurant and if, perchance, you find yourself in a place that matches its description, I suggest that you do not order the pommes frites.

26. Avignon

Like the North Magnetic Pole, the centre of power in Europe meanders erratically about. Sometimes it is in Paris, sometimes Vienna, sometimes Athens. For a brief time in the fourteenth century, it was in Avignon by the mighty river Rhône. Here, thanks to a schism in the Catholic Church, the Avignon popes set up their fabulous court. Underneath the grand assembly rooms of their palace is the treasury, and at its centre a great thick pillar, shaped like a tree and holding up the whole edifice. Only the Pope and the Treasurer were allowed into this room, to fertilise the tree with gold and silver.

Avignon, of course, also has its ancient bridge, although most of it was washed away in 1669, so that what is left behind is more like a pier; it projects about half way to a large island, the Ile de la Barthelasse, in the middle of the river, and then just stops.

In the nineteenth century Paul Boyton swam past here on his epic descent of the Rhône. Higher up the river he had, as usual, escaped death by inches. At a bridge on the Swiss French border a kind of portcullis had been lowered to prevent the smuggling of goods, its spikes pointing upriver. As Boyton approached this death trap, the crowd that inevitably lined the banks to cheer him on raised the alarm, soldiers laboured to raise the heavy barrier, and as he was swept inexorably forward, he just scraped beneath the barbs.

Shortly after arriving in Avignon, I set out confidently to swimhike beneath the arches of the bridge. This first effort to swim *sous le Pont d'Avignon* was a failure. I crossed the modern bridge to the island, jogged upstream, and entered the Rhône with the aim of swimming across to the bridge as I was pulled by the current under its nearest arch. My entry point was dictated by elementary mathematics. (a) I swim sideways at 2mph. (b) The river pulls me downstream at 4mph, so (c) by setting out a little over twice as far *above* the bridge than I am *across* from it: (d) under the arch I go.

Pont Daladier

Rhône

Île de la Barthelasse

City Walls

zebra

Avignon

Rue Ferrue

Rue René Rapide

Pont St Benezet

Place du Palais

Passage

Palais
des Papes

Cathedral

Rocher des Doms

Viewpoint

steps

steps

zebra

ferry

→N

100m

⟳ Entry: shallow with firm
mud → fringe of reeds →
steep rocky descent

The logic of this is impeccable, and if I had been entering a trigonometry exam rather than a river, I would have got full marks. But the Rhône had other ideas, or rather its flow was more complex than my calculation had allowed, because the water speeded up as it approached the bridge and I was swept past before I could reach it. Oops. Still, I ended up having a perfectly pleasant swimhike and if you want to have a go, and start out sufficiently high upstream you *might* reach the bridge from the island. However, *I do not recommend it*: you risk being run down by a barge.

I noticed that these barges were quite frequent later that day, after I had bought a ticket to walk along what is left of the bridge. My ticket came with an audio guide and whichever button I pressed, I always seemed to end up hearing some doleful warning about the turbulence and dangerousness of the river. Although I had been swimming in the Rhône that morning perfectly happily, this repeated insistence began to get to me. I looked at the eddies below the arches. They appeared harmless, but was this deceptive? Were they waiting to suck me down?

After an uneasy night, I set out the next morning with some trepidation. This time, I entered the Rhône from the Avignon side so it would be impossible to miss the arches, and everything went exactly to plan, apart from one curious incident.

I was swimming breaststroke and when I was a little above the bridge, I kicked something, something substantial, like a man's leg. As I swam on my quickly succeeding thoughts were these:

I have kicked something.
The thing I have kicked is *big*.
It does *not* feel like a log.
It feels like a leg.
It does not feel like a fish.
There are no crocodiles in the Rhône.

At this point my thoughts were interrupted when, from just behind me, came the sound of an ENORMOUS splash.

I have often wondered what it was that I kicked. Possibly it was a wels catfish. They are certainly big enough. But whatever it was had felt firm against my foot, where catfish are slippery. Also, of course, it had jumped out of the water and I am not sure that catfish do that kind of thing, even if they have been kicked. So, I think it was a second giant fish: a sturgeon. Sturgeon are thought to have been fished to extinction in the Rhône, with the last one caught in 1974. But their skin is leathery, and they jump.

The Building of Avignon Bridge
Around noon on the 13th September 1178 there is a total eclipse of the sun at Avignon. This is surely a sign from God! What might it portend? Anxious townsfolk flock to the cathedral where the bishop calms their fears. But his sermon is interrupted by a twelve-year-old shepherd boy called Bénézet, who strides down the aisle and announces confidently that the message of the eclipse is this: that people must come together to build a bridge across the Rhône. Bénézet is treated with sarcasm, and by some accounts is brutalised, before being ejected from the town, but he returns more determined than ever. By way of a joke, Bénézet is then told that if he wants to build a bridge, he should start with a great rock, almost the size of a boulder. To the amazement of the citizenry, he somehow manages to shift the rock into the river. Inspired by this apparent miracle, others join the lad, bringing further stones, and so the bridge begins. The enthusiasm spreads and soon the whole town is involved. Everyone plays their part according to their abilities and in 1185 the bridge is completed. Shortly before the bridge is finished, Bénézet dies, aged only 19. A chapel, which still stands, is built upon the bridge near the Avignon bank to house his body and there he is laid to rest. In 1669 the same flood that destroys most of the bridge carries Bénézet away in his coffin. But the body is recovered and when it is opened, he is found to be whole and incorrupt, his eyes still bright.

In this story Bénézet, like Cuthbert, is given that mark of sainthood: the body that remains pure and whole hundreds of years after death. But in contrast to the story of Cuthbert, where this miracle *is* the story: here it is a mere addendum to the account of how and why the Avignon bridge was built—and there is no doubt that it *was* built. As for Bénézet moving the great rock into the river to start the bridge, this 'miracle' was surely performed with help of the fulcrum by which Bénézet levered it onto a cart. By his intuitive grasp of mechanics, the boy himself becomes the fulcrum; he moves the whole town; his ingenuity—as well as his courage—is an inspiration to them. The townspeople realise that by shared effort, what seems impossible can be achieved. And so they combine as a community. The fame of the Avignon Bridge inspires others: associations of bridge builders, or pontiffs, are formed to span the other great rivers dividing Europe. In cooperation with the hospitalet, the inns, the pontiffs draw people together, make travellers safe, welcome the stranger. In these efforts to build bridges to connect people across natural boundaries lies the source of the idea of a united European continent.

For hundreds of years this marvellous and uplifting tale floated innocently down the stream of history, until it reached the modern age and was torpedoed by a submarine full of atheist historians ("a team of experts from many disciplines" explains the museum adjacent to the bridge). To their 'enlightened' eye there is nothing that inspires that cannot be reduced to material interests. So it is with the Bridge at Avignon. There was no communal coming together, no unifying idealism, the experts tell us with bleak satisfaction. No, it was all a base desire to extort tolls from the river traffic. Their argument for this depressing interpretation of why the bridge was built, such as it is, is an absence of evidence to support the traditional story. Now, in a way, this is true as the town records at Avignon were destroyed in the French Revolution but, by the same token, *there is no evidence for the atheists' story either.* There is no record of tolls being collected from boats at the bridge, nor of chains being attached between the arches to stop them from passing without paying. Furthermore, there is no physical evidence of any ring sockets or other modification in the stonework or design of the arches to allow for chains to be laid across them—as you can verify for yourself when you swimhike beneath them.

27. Marseilles

Before visiting Marseilles, I imagined it to be run-down and dangerous and full of thieves and prostitutes. But when I got there it wasn't, and I loved it. Marseilles is in many ways superior to Paris. The view from its Notre-Dame de la Garde is so breathtaking that it makes the view from the Sacre Coeur in Paris seem really rather ordinary. The museums are every bit as interesting; the natural history museum, in particular, is excellent. Outside there is a fantastical entrance by an impossible fountain-grotto featuring raging bulls. Inside, where many other museums have thrown away all their stuffed animals and replaced them with plastic dinosaurs, this museum has kept them, and where it *has* introduced plastic creations, these are not of dinosaurs but rather an exhibition of inter-animalia hybrids: insects on top and shapely nude women below. Outside the museum is a park, housing a zoo of plastic animals. Paris, it is true, has real ones in its zoo, but here again Marseilles shows itself to advantage, in being much less cruel. At night the Old Port is full of dancers and musicians, and in place of the Bassin de la Villette, there is the Mediterranean to swim in.

↻ The bays are about 2km south of the Old Port.

MEDITERRANEAN

Marseilles

Anse de Maldomé

steps

Traverse de la Cascade

Traverse Plaisance

beach

Anse de la Fausse Monnaie

John Fitzgerald Kennedy

Corniche du President

40m

→N

28. The Riviera

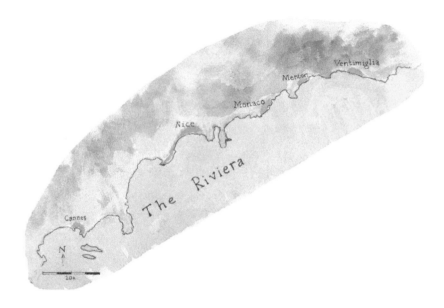

As a child, I found an illustrated book on the shelves of my grandparents. It was by Tove Jansson, and it included the story 'Moomin on the Riviera'. I loved this story. I was fascinated by the languorous lives of the wealthy characters, the gap between rich and poor, the casinos, the obsession with private property, the tiny bikinis, the hot relentless sun. I never went to the Riviera as a child; we spent all our holidays in Wales. But as soon as I could, I *did* go and discovered, to my delight, that it was *exactly* as Jansson had portrayed it.

Nice. There is a self-service bike hire scheme on the front, making swim riding possible...if you can work out how to follow the hiring instructions.

1. ↺ **Nice West** Enter: beach opposite Reu Lenval / Children's Hospital → swim west. Exit: little beach before airport →east on promenade.

2. ↺ **Nice East** East on promenade. Enter: beach opposite Negresco, west of boat access area → swim west. Exit: beach opposite Rue Lenval / Children' Hospital.

3. ↺ **Villefranche-Sur-Mer.** From Chapelle Cocteau skirt the Citadelle, follow a 'private' road to a carpark, then go *through* an anonymous building to join the coastal path, the Sentier du Littoral. These paths are everywhere along the coast of France. They were created by order of Napoleon and despite the continuing efforts of property owners to block them off, remain largely in place.

Enter: Pointe Sans-Culottes, just before the coastal path climbs to the road

Exit: beach below the Promenade des Professeurs harbour wall

4. ↻ **Cap Ferrat**. From Beaulieu-Sur-Mer take Promenade Maurice Rouvier to Saint-Jean-Cap-Ferrat. Uphill from its harbour is the Statue of the Mermaid with Perfect Breasts. Turn south for the Sentier du Littoral.

Enter: "Le Lido", a boomerang shaped apartment block southwest of Plage de Passable

Exit: Chiens Authorise Beach at southeast end of Villefranche beachfront.

5. ↻ **Saint Hospice**. From the church at Saint-Jean-Cap-Ferrat go uphill to the Mermaid and south on the Sentier du Littoral.

Enter: South of four stone struts

Exit: South west end of Saint Hospice Peninsula

Follow the Sentier dul Littoral around the Peninsula to Paloma Beach and return to the church by the road and pedestrian passage.

6. ↻ **Beaulieu-Sur-Mer**
From the station go south to the beach promenade.

Enter: west end of Beaulieu Beach
Exit: pebble beach framed by stone arch

Pass the 1909 tower and return to station via Rue Gallieni and Rue du Marché.

Monaco

29. Le Rocher

The British royal family can trace their ancestors back to 1066 and William the Conqueror. But the royal family of Monaco have a lineage that is almost as long. On a foul night in 1297, the gatekeepers of the fort at Le Rocher heard a tremulous knocking at the door. Outside stood a poor monk seeking shelter from the storm, so the kind-hearted guards let him in. How fateful it can be to answer—or not—to a knock! For the 'monk' was really the pirate chief Francois Grimaldi, also known as Grimaldi Malizia.* And as soon as the gate was opened, an armed band rushed in, killed everyone within, and seized the fort. Thus began the reign of the Grimaldi family who, on and off, have ruled Monaco ever since.

Whenever something sad happens to this family, the disreputable story of its origins is brought up to suggest that it is cursed. This, of course, is untrue: there is nothing particularly unusual about the founding of the Monaco dynasty for, as Thomas Paine points out, when you look into it, you discover that *all* monarchies begin with a band of ruffians. And it could hardly be considered unlucky to marry Grace Kelly, the perfect beauty and heroine of *High Noon*.

"Ah!" I would dream to myself. "If only Grace Kelly could have married *me*, rather than Will Kane (the hero portrayed by Cary Grant in the movie) or Prince Rainier (in real life)!" But I am not sure that it would have worked. Indeed, whenever I watch *High Noon*, despite my best efforts to identify with its hero, I cannot help but feel that my true sympathies lie with the man who hides in the back of his house when Kane comes knocking at the door.

---

* There is some disagreement over how to best translate this soubriquet. In the official histories of Monaco's monarchy, he is called Grimaldi the Cunning, but others refer to him as Grimaldi the Malicious, and Grimaldi the Spiteful. Perhaps the difficulty in choosing the correct term lies in the way that Grimaldi displayed *all* of these qualities.

I last visited Monaco in 2018 as an excursion from Beaulieu-Sur-Mer, where I was holidaying with my mother. Her dementia had advanced, but she could still take great pleasure from life. We both had a *fabulous* time on this vacation, and—more by luck than by judgement—I returned with her safe and in one piece.

The days of this precious holiday followed a fairly typical pattern. I crept out early to go swimhiking, and came back to find Mum awake and indignant that I had left her. We went down to the beach and had a swim, came back for breakfast eggs, and then set off to explore the area. Sometimes, I left Mum on a beach to go another swim, and if I did, she would berate me for abandoning her when I returned. In this stage of her illness, she lived and felt each moment intensely, but with little sense of past and future. (On our balcony, whenever a plane flew past on its approach to the airport, which happened every minute or so, she would see it afresh with interest and enjoyment, and point it out to me.) Anyway, I would defend myself robustly against the charge of desertion, stressing my extraordinary nobility in looking after her for 22 hours a day solid and was I not—pathetically—allowed a few minutes to myself? And we would have a loud histrionic argument. Then we would buy a whole roast chicken and bottle wine and eat it back at the flat.

Our final full day was, as usual, busy. After getting lost in Nice, we eventually found a bus back to Beaulieu and went to visit the Villa Greque Kerylos. The villa has a wonderful location giving views over the sea, and exquisite furniture, including its chairs, each with a notice which states that you are not allowed to sit on it. However, Mum was tired and sat on one, sat on its notice in fact.

"Mum, you can't sit there. There's a notice."
"Yes, I can. And there *isn't* a notice."

By the time we got back to our flat, Mum was very tired. She declined my optimistic suggestion that she might like another swim so I started making supper. Then she said something that sounded commonplace, but which, in her illness, astounded me:

"Would *you* like a swim Peter? *You* have one."

It was as a voice from the past, from when Mum understood that her children wanted to do their own thing, and wanted it too. So I did.

On our day in Monaco, my mother *came with me* on a swimhike. After taking the train there we walked circuitously down to Le Rocher and its *Musée océanographique*, a palatial building overlooking the sea that houses an aquarium and museum. Both are superb, but my mother was restless and we were soon back out in the heat of the day, taking the coastal track. We were not on this path by chance: I was looking out for the steps leading down to a beautiful little beach variously called Crique Ciappaira and Crique des Pêcheurs. I had seen this beach on a trip some years before but, frustratingly, had been unable to visit it. In my mind's eye, however, I had planned a small but aesthetically pleasing swimhike between this beach and the nearby concrete sundeck, and now I was going to take my chance to finally do it. Ah! Here it is! What a nice beach!

We are looking down at a sheltered cove; a moderate number of pleasant and wholesome looking couples and families have found it and are enjoying the sand and the water. It is the perfect place for me to leave my mother; while I take short swimhike, she can sit comfortably in the shade of the cliff.

Half way down the steps comes a jostle behind us. Teenage boys. We stand aside to let them pass.

"They didn't say thank you."
"It's OK Mum, they're German."

This comment was quite unfair—I have met many charming Germans—and ironic to boot as none are more notorious for their loutish behaviour while on holiday than the English. But I was vexed; it had all looked so nice, and now there seemed to be more and more of them clattering down behind us and pushing their way past. And they were decidedly not charming.

We find a spot near the base of the steps. More teenagers come rubbing past, surrounding us as we change into our bathing suits. We swim a little way out of the cove and I look back despairingly at the beach. Yet more uncouth young people have come pouring down the steps, so that the sand is now covered in a solid mass of obnoxious teenagers. With bitter disappointment I realise that I *can't* leave Mum there. I will just have to abandon my little swimhike. Then a daring thought strikes me—and why not? It is true that the

water can be wavy from the wake of boats, as landlords, drug dealers and oligarchs motor about in their superyachts. But even so, it is only about 200 metres, she can *easily* swim that. It is true too that the water becomes *very* deep, and my mother has never liked swimming out of her depth. But now, with dementia, *she doesn't mind at all.*

"Mum, would you like to come swimhiking with me today?"

Yes, she would. We swim back into the cove, where I leave Mum in the water and dodge my way back up the beach. Squeezing past the beefy youth who has commandeered our spot, I stuff Mum's towel and handbag into the top of the swimsac. That will do, I can pick up the rest later. Back down at the water's edge, at first I cannot see my mother. Surely, she could not have drowned as quickly as that? No, there she is in the shallows. I help her out into the deeper water and we set off. Mum swims over to the concrete sundeck perfectly competently, if very slowly. Now we just have to get out …up the ladder….Ah…the ladder… I hadn't thought about the ladder.

I demonstrate how to get out:

"Look Mum, it's easy. You just wait for the swell. Grab the rails, Climb up. And you're out! There." I unclip the swimsac and leaving it on the sundeck, jump back into the sea.

"Now you do it. I'll be right behind you."

I guide Mum into the ladder. She makes a fuss. She claims to be unable to move her feet. I swim beneath her and physically place her feet on the ladder. But now she says she cannot move at all. I swim down again, moving her feet up the rungs one by one, pushing her upwards until she is part way out the water. Now I get my shoulders beneath her and lift her up, step by step, carrying her up the ladder and out of the water. My mother is heavy but I feel nothing but determination and slowly raise her ever higher, until she gets her first foot on the concrete. Triumph! Her second foot reaches the concrete and she is out. Back on dry land! We have made it! Together! My mum: mother of five, legal scholar, magistrate, judge, and now *swimhiker!*

Italy

30. Ventimiglia

At Menton, on the French side of the border, the train stops for ten minutes while police prowl the carriages, eyeing each passenger in instant assessment. There had already been vague intimations that tourists were not the only travellers: who were all those black people corralled at the station in Nice? And then, from the train window, there seems to be some kind of camp at the water's edge with signs: "The world is ours to share." "We have human rights." The border is a pinch point for undocumented migrants, who are being kept off the trains at Ventimiglia, the final station in Italy. Some appear to be making a precarious living as street sellers in the market there, wrapping their goods in a blanket and hurrying away when the police appear. The police don't seem particularly anxious to chase after them, but occasionally they do make an arrest.

"It took four of them," explained Toshie who witnessed this. "I suppose they have to arrest at least one to show that they are doing their job."

The starting point of the Ventimiglia swimhike is also policed. Even early in the morning, the owners of sun umbrella territory defend their patch from interlopers. I am told by the young man putting out the deck chairs that I cannot leave my stuff here: the beach is private. Ha! I have no intention of leaving my stuff here. I am taking it with me. Once again, the swimsac shows its worth!

The route crosses the outlet of the Roya, which brings water straight down from the Alps to mingle with the Mediterranean. Around the mouth of the river, the sea becomes agitated; it sways, gulps, waves rise to a point and the temperature changes with surprising suddenness: warm, cold, warm again, cold again. Although the river is shallow, the effect is pronounced. (Is there a further subterranean source?) But eventually it goes away, and the swim ends in a calm bay protected by breakwaters.

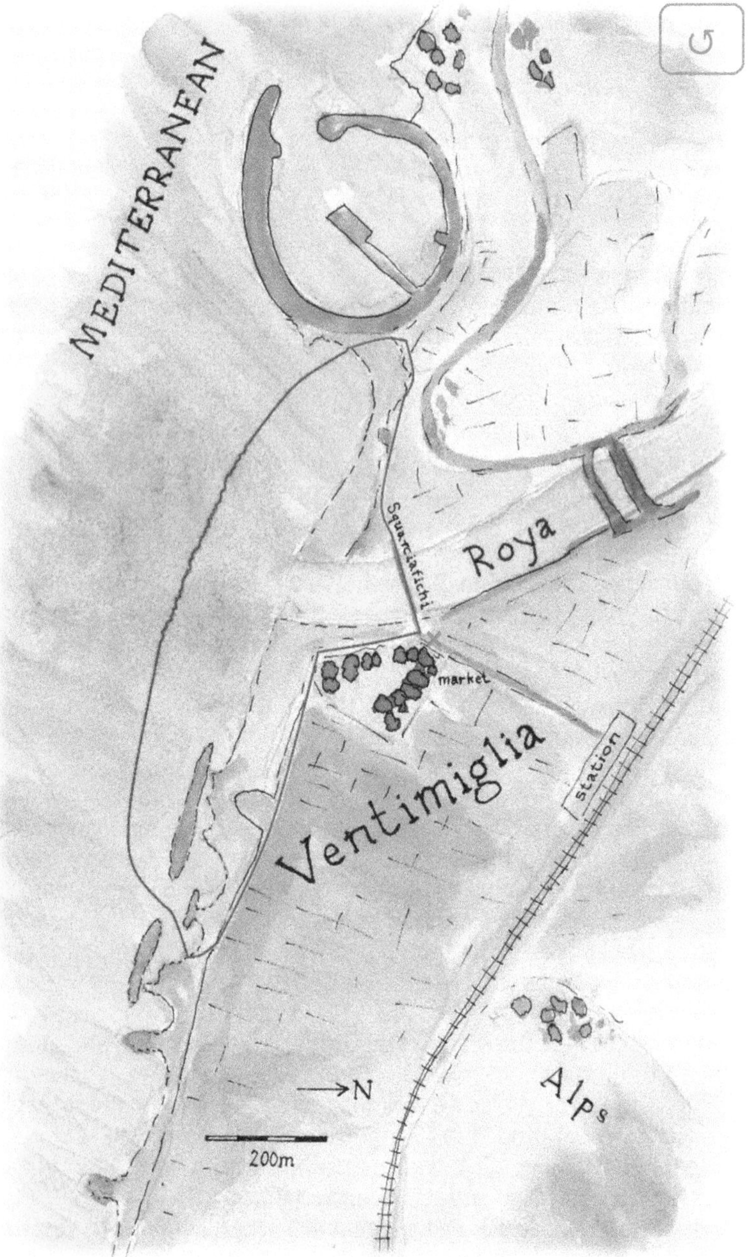

MEDITERRANEAN

Roya

Squiscialfichi

market

Ventimiglia

station

Alps

→N

200m

31. Stresa

Lake Maggiore

Stresa faces on to Lake Maggiore, where superb views set it up nicely to be the ideal tourist town. And so, in many ways, it is, although it is also curious in some respects. It has few footpaths, so you often have to walk in the roadway. It appears wealthy, and yet at least one in ten villas lie derelict, with dense jungles of palm and bamboo rising up around them in ghostly splendour. It also appears to have only one supermarket, and when I tried to go there it was shut. I search the empty streets for another in vain. All I can find are two wandering musicians, a trumpeter and an accordion player. I try and avoid them, but whenever I turn a corner, there they are again, playing right in front of me, cap out.

Swimhiking along the town's waterfront is very pleasant and works equally well in either direction, although swimming towards the northwest gives the best view of the Alps. Just to the southeast of the town, another swimhike loops around Villa Pallavicino Park, a combined zoo and botanical gardens, with interesting if low-key animals and fine grounds.

Next to Stresa are two islands: Isola Pescatori, the island-village, and Isola Bella, which has both a small village and an enormous palace, Palazzo Borromeo, built upon it. The islands are close by, so why not swim to them? Unfortunately, I decided that the speed boats buzzing between the islands and the shore made the trip too hazardous. I tried getting up early in the morning to avoid them,

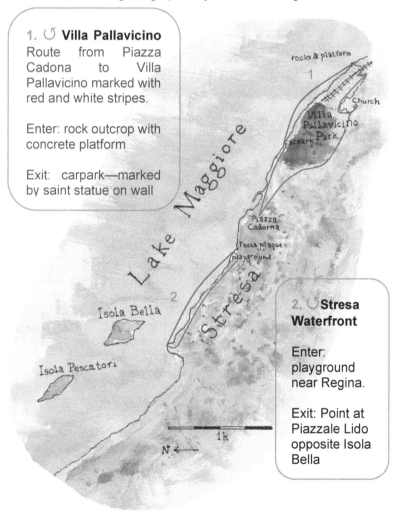

1. ↺ Villa Pallavicino
Route from Piazza Cadona to Villa Pallavicino marked with red and white stripes.

Enter: rock outcrop with concrete platform

Exit: carpark—marked by saint statue on wall

2. ↺ Stresa Waterfront

Enter: playground near Regina.

Exit: Point at Piazzale Lido opposite Isola Bella

only to find that *they* had got up early too and were already zooming about. So we visited the islands by boat, starting with Isola Pescatori.

The musicians must have come on the boat with us; we pass them in the village street where they greet me with smiles of recognition and cheerily hold out their hat. I pass by, stony faced, and we continue on to sit at a bench. The musicians come and sit on the adjacent bench and play, and play, and play. My hard-hearted attitude is obviously a challenge for them. We go to an open-air restaurant and order lunch. Shortly afterwards, they arrive there too, and start playing directly underneath us. But the wait for the food is so long that eventually they give up and wander off.

After wending our way through the narrow streets of the second island, Isola Bella, we enter its palace, and are signposted on a route through a hundred rooms. The rooms have high ceilings, windows that look over the lake, walls that are crammed with pictures, and rococo furnishings. Each room is more spectacular than the last, until you reach the final and most amazing room of all, one that is hung with ancient tapestries showing exotic African beasts, including two lions attacking a unicorn. After this comes the peaceful palace gardens, with doves and peacocks.

Back in Stresa, a plaque commemorates the occasion in 2013 when the central waterfront was renamed in honour of the Crown Prince of Dubai. I am a little unclear whether the waterfront is now called by the prince's full name, His Highness Sheikh Hamdan Bin Mohammed bin Rashid Al Maktoum, or by his preferred nickname, 'Fazza'. What makes the matter even more confusing, is that maps of the waterfront continue to show it as being named after Marconi. Anyway, the plaque explains that 'Fazza' identifies a person always willing to help others and to pass time with them, and that the Sheikh is full of feelings for the sufferings of his people and that there will be eternal brotherhood between his people and the people of Stresa and other things like that.

The Crown Prince was honoured, in particular, because of his contribution to powerboat racing. (Possibly this helps explain all the boats zooming about the lake.) On finding this out, I am struck by a sudden, glorious hope. If the people of Stresa have honoured His

Highness for powerboat racing, might they perhaps also want to honour *me* for my contribution to swimhiking? I would be happy with just a short bit of waterfront, a small piazza, or even a jetty. A cynic might reply that the only reason that the Crown Prince has the waterfront named after him is because he is wealthy, whereas I am not. However, as far as I can tell from the plaque and accompanying official pronouncements, Fazza's wealth has made *absolutely no difference* to the decision to honour him, which is rather entirely due to his simplicity and humility and warm heart. In short, as well as his contribution to powerboat racing, Fazza sounds really nice. There can be no doubt that *he* would have given the musicians some money.

Oh dear. The musicians: they gave me all those chances to show a bit of generosity, and yet I failed the test. With a sinking heart I finally comprehend the real reason why *I* will never get a plaque: I am too mean.

32. Venice

Venice is a tremendous city to explore, but it appears that the authorities there are not amenable to this exploration being undertaken by swimhiking. Projected onto the Campanile in Saint Mark's Square in illuminated letters are the instructions:

No Swimming
No Swimsuits
No Sitting on the Step and Eating
No Feeding the Pigeons.

These rules are enforced by tourist police and the Respect Venice Squad, so to avoid falling into their clutches we will retreat across the lagoon on the waterbus. This scenic boat trip has the main island of Venice on one side and the Isola di St Giorgio Maggiore on the other.* Its destination is the long low island strip that protects the city from the Adriatic: the Lido. From the Lido terminus, the broad outline of the swimhike is simple: hike east on the lagoon side, cut over to the Adriatic, and then take advantage of the prevailing current to the southwest to swim back along the beach until you reach the Blue Moon resort. Here you can get changed and—after having a picnic and feeding the pigeons—return down the main street to the ferry terminal. Try not to spread sand on the concrete pathways of the Blue Moon. I was at first rather careless about this: it is, after all, right on the edge of the beach. But there is a man whose job it is to sweep up this sand. And every day, when I came out of the sea, he would sigh so expressively as he followed me around with his broom, that eventually I started to feel rather guilty about it.

Back near St Mark's Square, a strange post box, a face with a wide frog-like mouth, edges the Doge's Palace. The post box was put there to allow Venetians to share incriminating information about

---

* St Giorgio Maggiore was the training ground for Nazi swimhikers. For their activities, see the discussion of the war hero John Bridge in *Swimhiking in the Lake District and North East England* 2nd Edition.

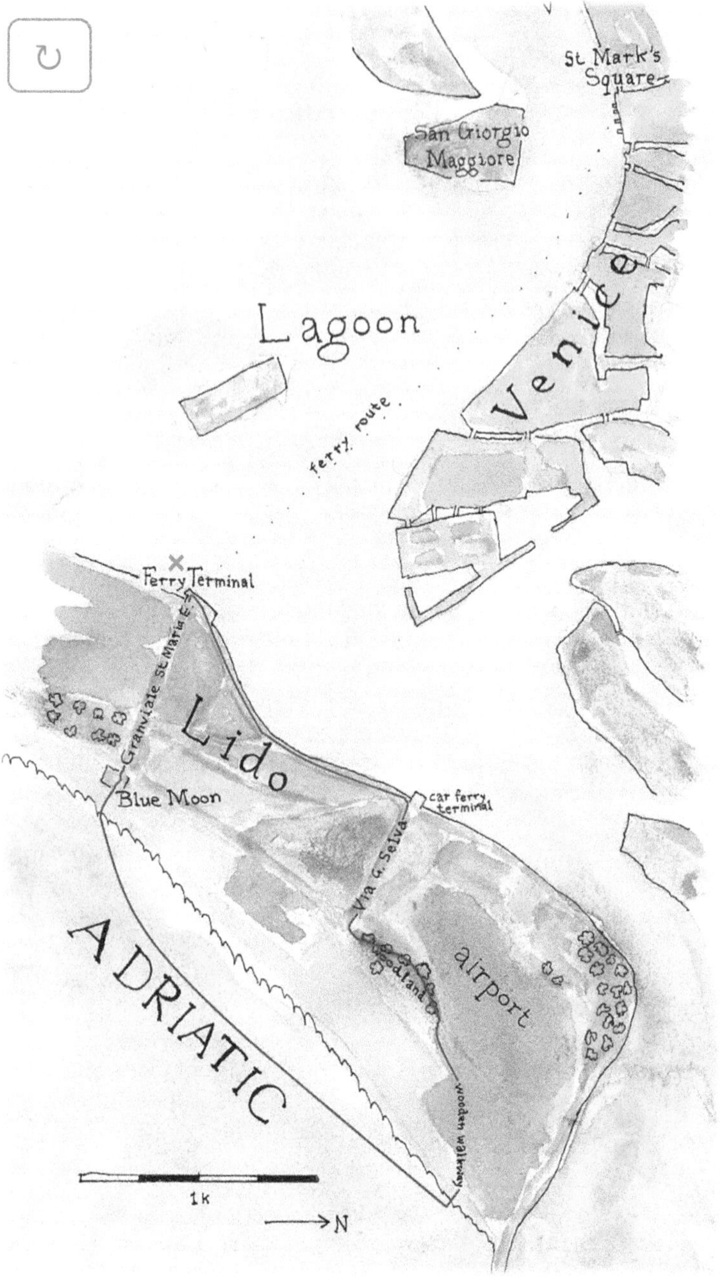

St Mark's Square

San Giorgio Maggiore

Lagoon

Venice

ferry route

× Ferry Terminal

Lido

Gran Viale S. Maria E.

Blue Moon

car ferry terminal

Via G. Selva

airport

A D R I A T I C

woodlands

woodland walkway

1 k

→ N

their neighbours. The mouth is still open and perhaps it can be conveniently put back into use to ensure that the unvaccinated who, in January 2022, were banned from the waterbuses, are obeying the rules and staying trapped on the surrounding islands. This prohibition may sound a little harsh but there are not really many places for them to go anyway, as they are also banned from pretty much all public venues. Still, for those of us who do not live in Italy this is all by the by. The only important issue is: *How do all these rules affect tourists like me?*

The Doge's Palace was the centre of power for the Venetians, controlling an empire that extended down the Adriatic to points eastwards all the way to Cyprus. At strategic places in between, fortified towns such as Split, and fortresses such as the one at Corfu, helped protect ships carrying tributes and trade into Venice from pirates, and extended the cultural achievements of Catholicism. And what incredible achievements these are! To take just one example, a little further along the front from the Doge's Palace is the church where Antonio Vivaldi was choirmaster. Here you can buy a ticket and listen to nightly concert performances of The Four Seasons.*

The fortified establishments of the Venetians were not just for spreading Catholic culture and fighting pirates. They also kept their Orthodox subjects in check and guarded against the Ottomans. The uneasy relationship between Catholic, Orthodox and Muslim, sometimes accommodating each other on friendly terms, sometimes falling on each other in savage wars, defines much of the politics of the region to this day. Now the tourist invasion is adding its own version of culture to these three great traditions. As scouts in this tourist army, we will swimhike our way past the relics of a turbulent history, looking up from the water to admire the sights and not worrying over much about all the blood that has flowed.

---

* There is no toilet available to the audience at these performances, but this does not matter over much because they do not last very long, as the musicians play all the movements, including the slow ones, *prestissimo*.

Croatia

There is an air of prosperity and order about Croatia, with few obvious signs of the terrible civil war that occurred as Yugoslavia broke apart. Near the beach at Trogir I notice an abandoned Orthodox church; in the Old Town of Split, a room honouring some of those killed; in the hills above Cavtat, some vague reference to landmines. But otherwise, there is nothing much. People do not seem to talk about the war, at least not with tourists, and you might forget about it altogether were it not for the feeling that the nationalism on display is just a little strident. Croatian flags are everywhere and they are, pointedly, often flown alongside flags of the EU, for Croatia is now part of the club, and their enemies are not.

33. Cavtat

The Racic family all died within a few years of one another, first the father, then the two children—of Spanish Flu—and finally the mother. Before she died, Mrs Racic arranged for them all to be reunited in their mausoleum at the top of the Rat Peninsula on the edge of Cavtat. This peninsula is delightful for walking and swimming and for swimhiking too, as you can pop in and out of the water at will. It is also possible to swimhike across the peninsula from the bays on each side.

Cavtat is at the southern end of Croatia. It lies next to 'Dubrovnik' Airport (which should really be called Cavtat Airport) and is only a few miles from the border with Serbia and Montenegro. The little town is pleasant for visitors to wander in and has a tourist information office, although for some queries, it is not an especially helpful one.

Tourist: Can you tell me how to get to Montenegro?
Tourist Information Lady: That is another country. You will have to ask them.

34. Split

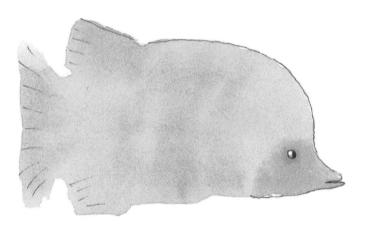

The waterfronts on both sides of the harbour at Split allow for very enjoyable swimhikes that simply involve swimming roughly along the line of buoys that separate swimmers from boats in one direction and walking back along the promenades. Looking up from the water, you see a dramatic mountainous coastline arising from behind the town; under the water, a mixture of rocks, sand and seagrass, and tens of thousands of fish.

Black Pasta
Toshie, Nicholas and I saunter along the harbour in Split admiring a line of posh superyachts. Their evenly spaced fenders have covers on them like a row of hats; handsome sailors scrub their already gleaming flanks. A little further on, past Zvončac Beach, we stop at an area of rocks with a ladder down into the water. As soon as you put your head beneath the waves, you encounter a gorgeous scene of teaming underwater life. However, entry is a little difficult: beneath the ladder is a shallow entry pool where the water is calm, but when a boat passes, the wake plays havoc.

"Come on in, the water's lovely," I say.
"I think I might keep my plastic sandals on," says Toshie.
"Don't bother: you don't need them."

Gingerly Toshie enters the water. A wretched superyacht zooms by.

"Quick!" I tell her, "Swim out into the open sea, before you get scraped on the rocks!"

Toshie swims out. Then she says "I can't put my feet down!" and swims straight back in again and puts her foot down on a sea urchin.

I help her out and run to look for a pair of tweezers. The first shop I come to is a supermarket.

"Do you have tweezers?"
"No."
"Do you know a shop where I might find them?"
"No."

But the very next shop is a pharmacy, which sells me two very expensive pairs of tweezers. Both pairs are quite useless at extracting sea urchin spines. The safety pin I use to secure my bumbag against thieves works a bit better, but it is not that good, as just when you think you are about to get a spine out, it breaks, leaving you digging down in a vain effort to lever out the remaining bit.

Eventually we manage to make our way to the hospital. It is a large complex, and all the directions are in Croat, but we make a good guess as to where to go and arrive at the reception. It is busy, but the one lady behind the desk appears to be remarkably efficient as we get to speak to her straight away.

"Yes?"
"My wife has trodden on a sea urchin. Can she see a nurse?"
"Yes. It happens all the time here. It happens to me too. Black Pasta. You need Black Pasta."
"What?"

"Black Pasta."
"Black Pasta?"
"Yes. Black Pasta. All the pharmacies know. There is one across the street. I will get you a needle." And she does.

We cross the street and ask for Black Pasta. From under the counter, the pharmacist pulls out a small tub, with Ihtamol written by hand on the label. It works remarkably well.

Nonetheless, our experience at the Split hospital seemed a bit haphazard. As far as I could tell, the woman at reception was not even a nurse, she was just a receptionist, so what business had *she* to go diagnosing our problems, giving us needles and instructing us on what to get from the pharmacy?* If we had been in *Britain* and gone to the NHS Accident and Emergency Department, I think things would have been done very differently. In fact, I know exactly what would have happened. We would have arrived and taken a ticket from the ticket machine, and after about 20 minutes we would have been 'triaged' and it would have been realised that our case was not an especially urgent one. Then we would have been placed in a special kind of queue, one in which—it would be virtuously explained to us—people are prioritised not according to when they arrive but in accordance with need. After about five hours waiting in this queue, we would have seen the doctor, and then we would have learned about Black Pasta and been sent on our way.

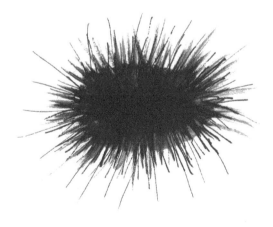

---

* I am, in fact, very grateful to this lady.

Bosnia

35. Mostar

The scenery is spectacular, but I do not care about the scenery, only the ache in my bladder. We are on the bus to Mostar from Split, and at the bus stop I had been too mean to pay 4 kuna to use the toilet. "There must be a toilet on the bus," I thought. But there isn't. However, in the seat pocket in front of me, someone has left a plastic bottle with a conveniently wide rim. When full it holds 500ml of liquid. Hmm. ... I realise that I simply do not know whether or not this is a sufficient capacity. But the sooner I find out, the more likely it is that it will be. In the next seat, Toshie has fallen asleep. The time is now! Seize the moment!

I take the bottle and unscrew the lid. The bottle is empty but, as if to thwart me, inside there is a specially designed system that I have never seen before. There is some kind of valve in there, and at its centre is a sharp plastic spike poking up towards the mouth. I push at the spike with my finger, trying to twist it to the side. Ouch! It *is* sharp, and no, that does not work. Well, maybe I can break it. Yes! The spike breaks with a sharp crack.

Toshie wakes up.

"What are you doing?"
"Oh, nothing."

Toshie immediately and correctly surmises my plan. Disapproves. Stays resolutely awake and alert for two hours as we crawl through traffic jams down the magnificent Dalmatian Coast. Finally, she drops off. Carefully, so as not to wake her, I manoeuvre the bottle, … insert, must get the angle right, now just relax and … But what is this? We are coming into a bus station.

"Ten minutes!" the driver announces. I extricate myself from the bottle, get off the bus and there, right in front of me, is the toilet. Fantastic! Entry costs 3 kuna but—even better—the lady is not there, so my wee is free, and more than 500ml I think.

At the next stop, a couple of hours later, the toilet is guarded by Rosa Klebb. I pay her and go again. I have changed my mind about paying.

In Bosnia the wounds of war are still apparent. The country is *de facto* split into two: Bosnia Hercegovina and The Republic of Srpska. There are bullet holes in the walls. There are genocide museums in both Sarajevo and in Mostar, and the people who live there tell stories of what happened.

Mostar's ancient bridge, built high over the Neretva river by the Ottomans in 1566, was destroyed in the war but has now been rebuilt. It was not just the bridge that was ruined in the conflict. Before the war, the city was integrated, many people intermarried and did not define themselves by ethnic labels, happy enough to be

Yugoslav. Now the curse of ethnic identity is mapped into the geography of the city. On one side of the bridge are Muslim Bosniaks, on the other, Catholic Croats. And the Orthodox Serbs that used to live there before the war? The city has been 'cleansed'; they are gone.

By walking beneath a small and charming waterfall and then edging along a narrow track beneath the Old Bridge, you can enter the river above it and swim downstream. The Mostar Diving Club jumps from the bridge, so watch out! And the water is *cold*.

From Mostar, a spectacular train journey along the Neretva Gorge ends in Sarajevo. Here, by the Latin Bridge, Frantz Ferdinand and his wife were shot and the First World War set in motion. However, the river Miljacka beneath looks rather shallow, so you can't really swim underneath *this* bridge. Swimhikers, therefore, will want to take a second trip, by road, to the Kravica Falls.

Old Bridge, Mostar

36. Kravica

The lower waterfalls at Kravica are a fine sight, and the upper falls are indescribably beautiful. If you can, at least once in your life, you should make a pilgrimage there. To swimhike between the falls, enter the water just below the upper falls and swim down the Trebižat river. At one point there are some gentle rapids to negotiate, but for the rest, the river is deep. Once beneath the modern road bridge, be on the alert: you will soon arrive at a rocky island just above the lower falls where, naturally, you will want to get out. Then walk back eating figs.

We had hired someone to drive us to the waterfalls and on the return journey, he asked us if we had any questions.

"Yes. There was a sign at the waterfalls, in several languages, saying religious rituals are prohibited. Why?"

"Ah, yes, that was the Saudis. Two years ago [in 2016], they started to pray there. They would bring their carpets down. That was OK. But then they said, 'Why are you there flaunting your bodies in this holy site?' But people go there to swim; it is a place to swim, not to pray. And there were fights. So they put up the sign."

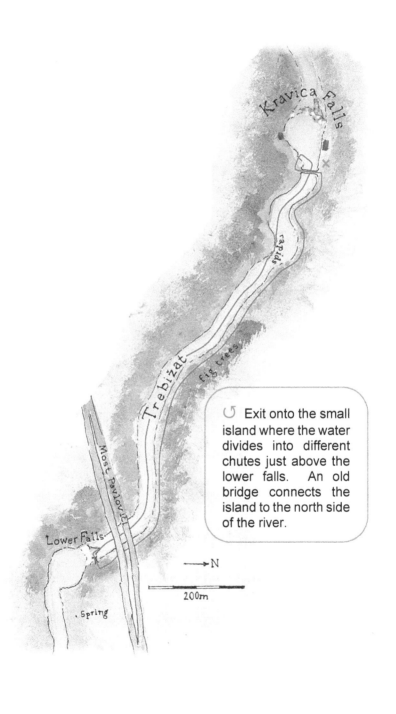

Kravica Falls

rapids

Trebižat

fig trees

Most Pavlović

Lower Falls

Spring

↺ Exit onto the small island where the water divides into different chutes just above the lower falls. An old bridge connects the island to the north side of the river.

⟶ N

200m

Greece

37. Corfu

Old Fortress

When Corfu belonged to the Venetians, they built a huge spiky fort on the peninsula by the main town, cutting a channel to make it an island. You can cross the bridge to visit the historic buildings inside the fortress, and climb to the high point where swallowtail butterflies dance. You can also explore the fort in a swimhike starting from Garitsa Bay. From the calm beginnings of the bay, the cliffs of the peninsula become ever more dramatic, and the sea, which is generally shallow on this side of the island, becomes deep and blue. Past the main point of the peninsula is a further outcrop, a striated line of white cliffs to swim around, before turning back into the gentler waters on the north side of the fortress, a lion relief on its outer wall. Get out onto the beach before the harbour, where a path under arches takes you into the fort, from here you can wend your way to the bridge and back into the town.

Next to the bridge into the Old Fort is a statue to Johann Matthias von der Schulenburg, who led the defence of Corfu when it was besieged by the Ottomans in 1716. Each year, on Saint Spyridon's Day, a ceremony at the statue commemorates how he saved the island with the help of the saint who, more than a thousand years after his death, came back to life and helped to scare the Turks off. Nearby, there is a bust to Gerald Durrell, the writer and zookeeper who grew up in Corfu. Durrell's nose is quite a different colour from the rest of his face, as it has been rubbed golden by countless hands. Perhaps rubbing his nose is thought to bring good luck, or perhaps a collective effort has been made to change its colour merely for the sake of entertainment.

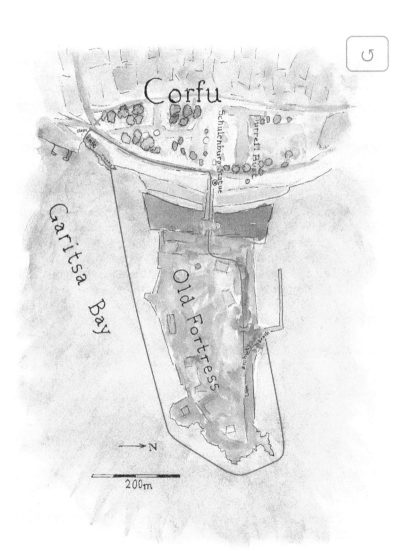

Corfu

Schulenburg Statue

Burret Bust

Garitsa Bay

Old Fortress

→N

200m

Mon Repos

When Corfu belonged to the British, they created a great wooded estate just south of the main town complete with a large villa, built on the lines of a stately home, called Mon Repos. The villa is famous—at least as far as guidebooks are concerned—as the birthplace of Prince Philip, although there are some gaps in the record of exactly what happened. By common consent, the prince was born on a table, but accounts vary as to whether this was the *kitchen* table or the *dining room* table. There is also a general consensus that the table was chosen on the advice of a doctor, but there is only silence on *why* the doctor gave this advice. Unfortunately, the museum that is now housed in the Mon Repos villa does not answer these questions, and in fact makes no mention of Prince Philip at all. What, then, can be deduced from what we know? First, for reasons of propriety, the prince should surely have been delivered on the dining room table, which must have been quite a grand one, probably of polished mahogany. A *kitchen* table, by contrast, simply sounds common. And yet...and yet, Prince Philip *did* have something of the common touch about him. He made jokes that—although you weren't *meant* to like them—were often quite funny. At least I found them so. As for the doctor's advice, one can only presume that he suggested a table when concerns were raised about making a mess on the bed. This lends further support to the theory that the prince was delivered on the kitchen table, because you would, naturally, not want a grand dining room table to get messy either.

In the grounds of Mon Repos are relics of antiquity, including a magical glade with a Doric temple. The beach nearby has a delicious spring to drink from before embarking on swims through shallow water north to the windmill at the end of Garitsa Bay, or south to the picturesque Vlacherna Monastery and Church, on an island connected to the land by a breakwater. After climbing the hill that overlooks the church, you can pause at the café to watch planes coming in *underneath* you to land at the airport.

Garitsa Bay

Windmill

Basilica
Palaiopólis

Mon Repos Estate

Mon Repos

Hera
Sanctuary   Spring

Doric
Temple

1. ↺ Windmill

2. ↻ Church

cafe
steps

Church

N

400m

Paleokastritsa

Octopus beneath the cliff at Paleokastritsa

I must have been nervous about planning to undertake an early morning swimhike beneath the great cliffs of Paleokastritsa, as I am secretly relieved when I learn that I will not, after all, be able to. The weather is just too bad. There is snow. Seven centimetres of snow, with up to thirty centimetres forecast. Unusual to have snow in Greece in July.

I jerk awake. It is 5.58am. It is time to go.

As it turns out, the swimhike around the cliffs, caves and rocks of Paleokastritsa, while very beautiful, is entirely uneventful and I get back in good time for breakfast with my mother, before another day of swimming and walking. Our favourite hike is up to the Paleokastritsa Monastery to enjoy the views, the flowering trees, the beehives and the genial priests in its grounds. We also enjoy watching the tortuous movements of the cars that, rather than parking in the enormous carpark at the base of the hill, drive up the narrow winding road to the top in the hope that they can park right next to the monastery, and then discover that they cannot.

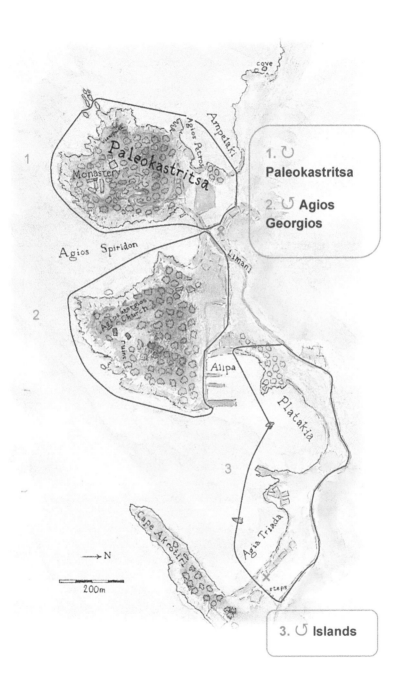

cove

1

Ampelaki

Agios Petros

Paleokastritsa

viewpoint

Monastery

1. ↻
Paleokastritsa

2. ↻ **Agios
Georgios**

Agios Spiridon

Limani

2

Agios Georgios
Church

ruins

Alipa

Platakia

3

Cape Akrotiri

→N

200m

Agia Triada

steps

3. ↻ **Islands**

38. Athens

Central Athens is teaming with tourists marvelling at the achievements of the ancients. Everywhere are amazing sights ringed with people holding up phone cameras. In a rare moment of calm, we see a wild tortoise walking placidly over the site of the Temple of Aries. There is nobody else there, and in a past age we might have been content to watch its progress in silent wonder, but this being the twenty first century, we film it. Then the tortoise is gone, and we return to the noise and the madding crowd.

Eventually, you will no doubt feel the need to take a break from all this and go swimhiking. One option is to go to the port of Piraeus and catch an island ferry, but another is simply to take the tram from Syntagma Square to the Asklipiio Voulas terminus. The tram was built for the 2004 Olympics. It is smooth and air conditioned and is relaxing to ride on. The only difficulty is the highly advanced ticket machine which—like so many modern ticket machines—is *so* highly advanced that it is almost impossible to use. Once at the terminal, you can pay a modest fee to access the pleasant facilities at South Beach.

There is, however, no need to pay to reach the sea.* Just north of the beach resort, a ruined ticket booth marks an open gateway and a path that wends its way past various other modern ruins to a public beach. It is, in fact, the same beach as the pay beach, separated by a line of flags. At the north end of this beach, wade around the fence to the Model Beach for People with Disabilities. (I am very much in favour of providing people with disabilities with facilities to access the coast and countryside, but they do not need to be cut off from everyone else.) After crossing this beach, you can now walk out on a short peninsula to a knoll that provides a fine view of the Athenian coastline. Beneath the knoll is a pill box, steep steps leading you down into it. And below on the south side, a sheltered cove of pebbles. From here you can swim back to the public beach while looking down at an underwater world of red starfish, black sea urchins, big round black sponges, and vivid green and blue fish.

---

* You might feel that it is out of character for me to pay to visit a beach. However, I did so because if I did not, a friendly Greek gentleman, who was telling me how nice it was inside the place, was insisting on paying the entrance fee for me.

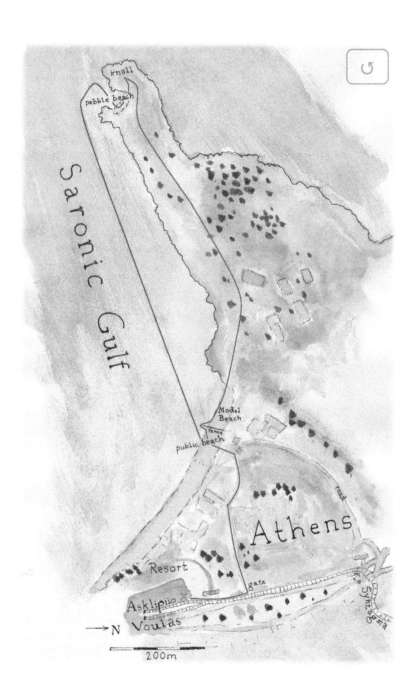

39. Hydra

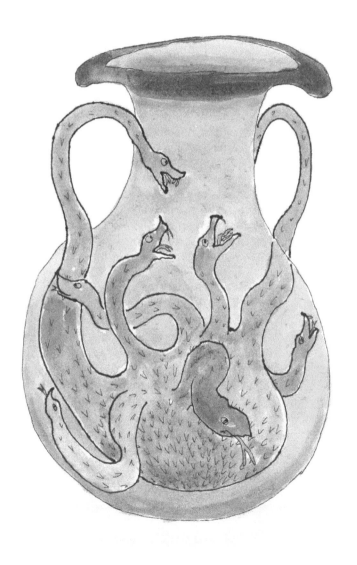

Boats to the Greek Islands have a movie-poetry about them: they are antiquated and slow, and are crowded with *real people*, invariably including someone transporting chickens. In my experience, the ferries from Piraeus are indeed often crowded and although I have never noticed any chickens, there is an atmosphere of a sort created by all the cigarette smoke. Also, it does seem to take a long time for the ferries to get anywhere, but this is compensated for by the great view from on deck as they chug interminably along. The boat to Hydra is completely different. Very modern. Fully enclosed. Sleek and fast, Comfortable temperature. Comfortable seats. Impossible to go outside. Few bother looking at the view; many draw the curtains. And soon we are there.

Hydra is a well-heeled and sunny place for tourists. It has a museum that celebrates the fight to get rid of the Ottomans, mysterious orthodox processions, a monastery like an eyrie sticking out precariously from a cliff in the centre of the island, and an arid landscape—with large bottles of water imported from the mainland stacked on the dock. And it is true! No cars, only mules and donkeys and going by foot. Wonderful! Unfortunately, the same enlightened rule does not extend to the surrounding sea, where there are a lot of fast moving water taxis.

Hydra means water, but as there is hardly any fresh water to be had, giving the island such a name seems odd. Archaeologists claim to have found one or two stone channels in which water was gathered. However, the fact that there might have been efforts to collect what little water there was, is hardly very convincing as an etymological explanation for the island's name; it is surely more likely that the name was given in irony, like the name of Robin Hood's companion Little John. Alternatively, a many headed monster called the Hydra lived in a swamp not *that* far away in the Lerna Marshes on the Peloponnese peninsula. Can this be mere coincidence? It is easy to imagine that a large octopus frequenting, say, the island's harbour, was confused with sightings of the beast.

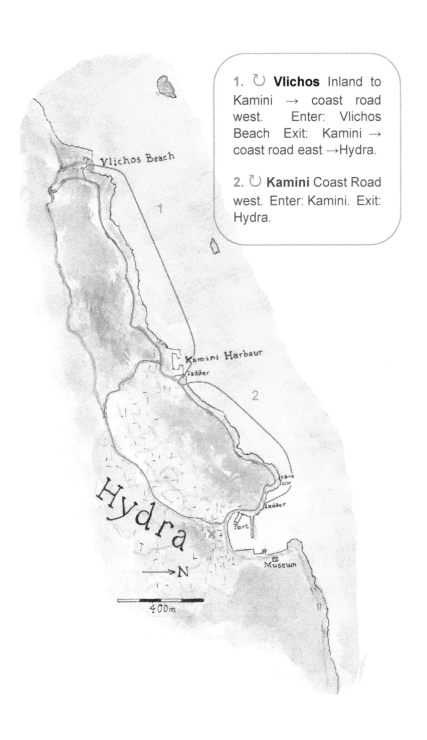

1. ↺ **Vlichos** Inland to Kamini → coast road west. Enter: Vlichos Beach Exit: Kamini → coast road east →Hydra.

2. ↺ **Kamini** Coast Road west. Enter: Kamini. Exit: Hydra.

Vlichos Beach

1

Kamini Harbour
ladder

2

cave

ladder

Port

Hydra

X

→N

400m

Museum

Turkey

40. Olu Deniz

Bay at Olu Deniz

There is no need to describe the view of Olu Deniz in any detail because holiday features on Turkey always provide its picture: a big fat finger of beach, its bulbous tip pointing to steep green hills on the far side of a narrow channel. On one side of the beach is the open water of the Mediterranean; the other side has been christened the Blue Lagoon, although 'Olu Deniz' actually means 'Dead Sea'. Because it is so famous, the beach apparently becomes crowded with thousands of people who, having seen the photo, think 'Ooh! That looks nice. I will go there'. And one Easter, when we found a bargain holiday only two miles down the coast, we were most excited to be joining them. However, whenever I visited Olu Deniz beach it was entirely empty of tourists, although this is not to say that there was no one there.

On our first morning, before breakfast, I set out to explore from our hotel, a huge complex full of swimming pools, lawns, shady groves and amphitheatres, all surrounded by a barbed wire fence. It was

Heaven with just a touch of Guantanamo Bay. However, where the barbed wire fence met the sea, it was possible to clamber around

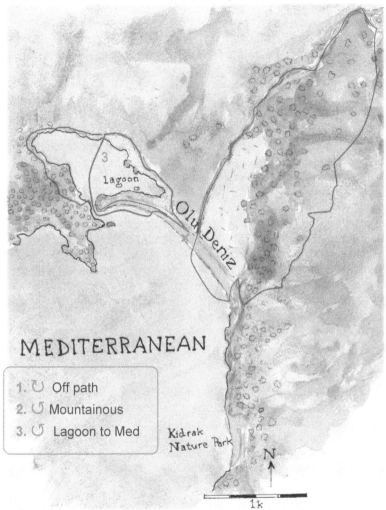

MEDITERRANEAN

1. ↻ Off path
2. ↻ Mountainous
3. ↻ Lagoon to Med

Kidrak
Nature Park

N

1k

it to escape the hotel grounds onto the next beach. This beach was called Kidrak Nature Park and it was protected by *another* barbed wire fence, quite an effective one. However, by engaging in a bit of low level rock climbing at the far end, it was possible to circumvent the fence to reach the coast road leading to Olu Deniz. Having got to this road and explored a bit, I turned back and retraced my steps.

On Kidrak Beach a group of men had arrived in a minibus, and one hailed me as I jogged along the shoreline. He told me, very politely, that the beach was not open and that I was not allowed on it. He warned me, again very politely, not to enter the beach again, and wished me a happy holiday. The next morning, I heeded his advice and set out for Olu Deniz on the road. I noticed as I passed the Kidrak Nature Park that it now had a guard dog.

Two thirds of Olu Deniz beach is public, but when you reach the final third, the top joint of the finger that juts into the famous lagoon, there is a fence that extends partly down the beach, and a sign board. On the sign is a polite notice which says that before going further, please purchase a ticket. I had been forewarned that you had to pay, and had some money with me, but as I could not see anyone to buy a ticket from, I kept going. It was early in the morning and early in the season, and I assumed the ticket collectors had not yet arrived. As I ran on, I began to hear a kind of squawking noise behind me. I decided to ignore it and kept going; it could, after all, be some kind of seagull, or perhaps a goose, but after the noise changed to an angry shout, I could not very well ignore it any longer. The man came stumping up to me and, with considerably less politeness than the man the day before, told me that if I wanted to run down the beach, I had to buy a ticket.

"OK."
"Four lira."

I obligingly whipped out a five lira note. He took it and shooed me off. I must wait for him further down the beach.

I found him again on the lagoon side, morosely pulling an empty fishing line out of the Dead Sea. He went away and duly came back with my ticket and change.

From the point of the finger beach, I looked across to the forest and steep rocky shoreline on the far bank. There was a duck house and a sign in Turkish, but no sign of a path. A little way down, however, was a shallow inlet with a bit of beach that I thought might provide a way in to the woods. I swam for the inlet, swimsac on my back. As I neared the other side, I could hear the noise of a boat being launched somewhere behind me. I did not look round, but quickened my stroke to the far bank, changed as quickly as I could and pushed up through the trees and undergrowth to be out of reach of authority.

Once out of sight of the shore, I relaxed and began to enjoy the wilderness. The way was tricky with thorns, but not impassable. At the summit of the hill, two stones served as a cairn, so someone had been before. Everything was still apart from the bees that buzzed everywhere.

My plan was to make my way through the forest to reach the road that skirted the inland side of the lagoon, but the going became increasingly rough. I attempted to descend to the lagoon so that I could swim there, but the bushes pressed closer, and the slope became progressively steeper. I was thinking I might have to go back when, to my delight, I found a miniscule goat track, so small that had my eyes not adjusted to search for the tiniest semblance of a path, I would not have noticed it at all. It wended through the bushes and under low hanging trees to the ruins of a stone hut, perhaps an outlier of the "abandoned" (in fact 'cleansed') Greek village of Levissi a few miles inland. Beyond the hut lay a marsh at the end of the lagoon. And on its far side was a bit more scrub and then the dirt road. I had made it! All of a sudden, my legs began to sting from all the scratches. Until then, intense concentration had made me oblivious to them.

I returned to the hotel where, after I showed my pass, the guard let me in. Back at the room, I found that my hair was full of twigs.

On the way back along the road, I had noticed a triangular hiking sign and some steps leading up the mountain, so the next day I went to see where they went. The steps quickly ended and there was no path, but there were blobs of green paint to follow, perhaps every five yards. The blobs took me up the mountain to a large ravine and cliff that appeared impassable. Here the blobs squeezed in together, sometimes only a few inches apart, to guide me very precisely over the drop. A little way higher, the blobs entered a wood and then disappeared under the scree of a recently cut dirt road that joined the main road down to the tourist town, where I completed the loop with a swim along the public beach.

Neither of these swimhikes could I wholeheartedly recommend. The first was too scratchy, the second too steep. But I had in mind a third route: I would go back to the finger beach, but this time I would avoid the forest by swimming right across the middle of the lagoon from the tip of the finger all the way to the road.

The next morning, I went straight to the official ticket booth, for I now knew where it was. Three men sat outside the turnstiles and one rose to greet me. I scrabbled in the swimsac, took out my money and offered it to him. The beach was closed. It opened in twenty minutes, at eight o'clock. The man went and sat down again.

To fill time, I ran disconsolately down the dirt road that skirted the inland side of the lagoon, wondering if I dared to do the route the other way around, thus landing on the finger beach *without a ticket*. On the whole, I thought not.

Below, the lagoon lay still and empty. It was very tempting, and there was certainly no harm in just a quick swim. Then, as I changed into my swimsuit, an ambitious plan formed in my mind. I would swimhike across the lagoon. But would *not* get out on the nearside of the finger beach where a ticket was required. Instead, I would swim straight on through the narrow channel and out to the open sea. Then I would *keep on swimming* until I reached the sign that marked the border with the public beach. Only then would I get out.

I entered the warm green cloudy water and swam towards the channel. Shoals of small fish skitted as a larger fish took a lunging gulp. The lagoon was completely calm and full of little soft bumpy things. They were tiny jellyfish. Olu Deniz, I suppose, must be one of the places they go in the winter to shelter, before heading out to colonise the Mediterranean in the summer. Their stings were imperceptible except on the delicate skin of my inner forearm, where I could just feel them.

I swam by the inlet from my first swimhike and the water became suddenly colder. I only now realised how warm it had been in the shelter of the lagoon.

I was almost at the narrow channel that would take me past the fingertip of the beach, when I was spotted. A man in black launched a pedalo, paddled urgently towards me. Could I outswim a pedalo? Probably not. I decided to ignore him. He drew closer and slowed down, saying nothing but positioning his boat between me and the finger beach. The sea was getting colder in stages and becoming more wavy until I reached the open water, where the man in black turned round and pedalled back into the lagoon.

The water was not truly cold, but it *felt* cold because I had been spoiled by the lagoon. Down the outer shore, the signpost that marked the border with the public beach looked a long way away, and the sea was choppy. Should I get out now? I had already swum further than I had originally planned, I was chilly, and the beach appeared deserted. I wavered. Could they *really* be still there, hidden in the bushes, creeping stealthily along, ready to pounce the moment that I landed? How absurd! I began to laugh at myself at this paranoia.

A man appeared out of the undergrowth. He walked down the sand to the sign that divided the private beach from the public beach and stood there grimly, cutting off my exit if I landed. That decided it. I would swim until I reached the sign, I would indeed swim a little way *past* the sign, to make absolutely sure that I got out on the right side of it.

The man stared at me intently until I was a few yards from the sign, then turned on his heel and walked away. A second man now appeared from the bushes and the two of them had an altercation. Perhaps the first man was being upbraided for breaking cover. He turned and pointed forcefully towards the sign, though I could not tell if this gesture for me or for the man he was arguing with.

I got out on the public beach, curious to know if I would be asked to buy a ticket for swimming in the sea. I was not. Whether this was because I was not in fact required to have a ticket, or whether once I was on the public beach I could claim sanctuary and refuse to pay, I do not know. However, I do know that I found this last swimhike especially satisfying and recommend it to anyone visiting Olu Deniz.

Cyprus

41. Protaras

Dotted around Cyprus are many fine sights dating back to antiquity. I will not list them. Suffice it to say that, yes, all these mosaics, sculptures, shrines, temples, churches and mosques, are well and good, but they do not tell us what cultural artifacts will have been created by *our* invasion: the tourist invasion. Fig Tree Bay, at Protaras in southeast Cyprus, probably provides as good an answer as any to this question. We have the hotels there, of course, and on the beach we have the sun umbrellas, spaced at precise intervals, the upturned shields of a Roman legion. And we have our special tourist flag, the Blue Flag, flapping proudly in the breeze to show that the resort has met 'the gold standard for beaches' etc etc. And like all too many beaches living up to this gold standard, it is full of jet skis.

I wrote to the Blue Flag organisation suggesting that the jet skis that litter their beaches and menace its swimmers are incompatible with any number of their 'rules', including keeping vehicles off the beach; protecting the nature, atmosphere and aesthetics of the place; preventing noise nuisance, and not disturbing wildlife. They replied to say they would hold a meeting about it and let me know the outcome. And that was the last I heard.

One sight in Cyprus is rather unusual: the mosque that was once Saint Sophia's Cathedral. While cathedrals in Western Europe were having their statues and stained glass windows smashed up in the Protestant Reformation, something similar was happening in the East. In 1571, the Ottomans invaded Venetian Cyprus. They captured Nicosia, and while its inhabitants were being variously tortured, massacred and enslaved, they also rapidly stripped Saint Sophia's of its choir, altars, statues and stained glass windows and declared it a mosque. It is still a mosque today, and as a tourist you are welcome to pay a visit. However, Cyprus is a divided island, with a fence separating the North from the South (one that has lasted longer than the Berlin Wall and shows no sign of going away). This fence runs through Nicosia, and as the one-time-cathedral is in the northern half, to reach it from the South you have to pass through the border crossing and enter The Turkish Republic of Northern Cyprus. Once across, the mosque is easy to find, and soon you will be taking off your shoes and going inside. It is a strange and unsettling experience. The building has the familiar dimensions and acoustics of a cathedral, but it *is* a mosque with whitewashed interior walls, carpeted floors, austere. It has new inhabitants, yet still the architecture whispers of its ghostly Christian shell.

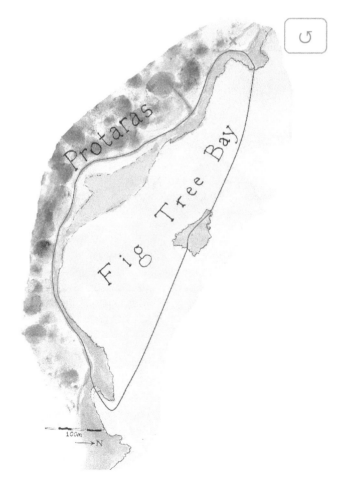

Spain

42. Menorca

Pont d'en Gill

For the most part, Menorcans have managed to defend their island against the throbbing tourist hells that scar so much of Spain's beautiful coastline. But in one arid little corner, near the town of Ciutadella on the western side of the island, a hideous tourist 'development' has been allowed to run riot. Guidebooks pass over this place in pained silence, or scathing one-liners. But when we went one summer we loved it, me especially. Its cliffs are largely choked off by holidays villas on land, but when seen from the sea they are varied and beautiful. There is a striking natural arch, the Pont d'en Gil. Best of all, the cliffs are intersected with *calas*, narrow fjord-like inlets that makes the area *perfect* for swimhiking. At least, it would be perfect, were it not for the fact that its annual influx of holidaymakers coincides with its annual influx of jellyfish.

I first encounter Menorca's infamous jellyfish early one morning when half way between Cala en Brut and Cala en Blanes. I have found a gap between the greedy coast grabbing villas and taken a ladder down into the deep blue water. Now I am happily swimhiking beneath the cliffs. The current pushes me where I want to go and I am thinking "Isn't this idyllic" when,

"Ouch!'

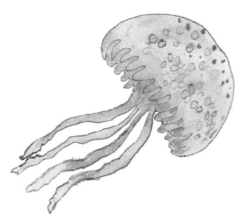

I am stung on the arm. Peering under the water I find that I am amidst a school of jellyfish, small and brown with distinct thick tendrils that make them look almost like squid. They are *Pelagia Noctiluca,* also known as the Mauve Stinger. I slow down, trying to avoid them, but they are *everywhere.* It feels like a video game that gets progressively worse. I try striking out to sea. They keep coming.

"Ouch!"

I am in a quandary. Should I go *further* out to sea? But what if there are even more out there? Should I go back to Cala en Brut? But then I would have to swim through them again, this time against the current. Should I keep going? But then what if they get worse...

"Ouch!"

The rising sun makes the decision for me. I have been looking underwater to try and avoid the jellyfish (another dilemma as it risks a sting in the face), but now the sun climbs above the cliff and blinds my view. So as to see, I swim up close against the cliff where the water is still in shadow. I peer beneath the water; the jellyfish are gone. Hugging the line of the cliff, I swim nervously round the final point and into Cala en Blanes.

As chance would have it, swimming in towards a cliff when surrounded by jellyfish is a good choice. Despite being so often washed up on the beach, jellyfish do not, as you might think, float

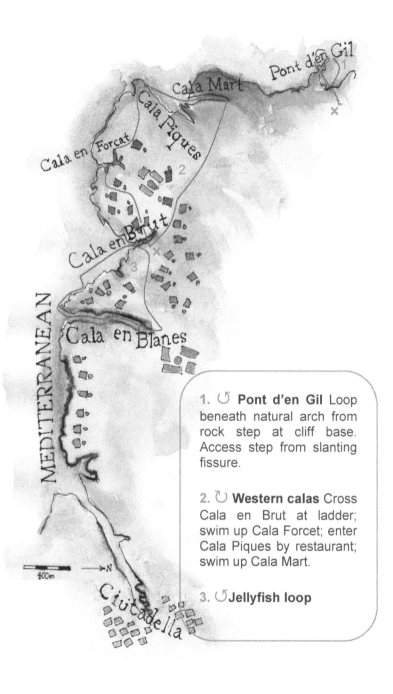

Pont d'en Gil

Cala Mart

Cala Piques

Cala en Forcat

2

Cala en Brut

×

3

MEDITERRANEAN

Cala en Blanes

×

400m →N

Ciutadella

1. ↺ **Pont d'en Gil** Loop beneath natural arch from rock step at cliff base. Access step from slanting fissure.

2. ↻ **Western calas** Cross Cala en Brut at ladder; swim up Cala Forcet; enter Cala Piques by restaurant; swim up Cala Mart.

3. ↺ **Jellyfish loop**

around helplessly wherever the sea takes them, but swim quite deliberately using a variety of complex motions that propel them through the water with remarkable efficiency. Because they swim deliberately, they naturally do their best to avoid rocks and cliffs where they might be battered about. *How* they decide to avoid rocks and cliffs is a mystery to scientists. Indeed, even their very *ability* to swim cannot be explained by science. As a matter of fact, for all their rather conceited view of themselves as knowing much more than ordinary folk, scientists cannot actually explain how *any* organism, whether a jellyfish or a human being, *chooses* to swim from one place to another. Of course, they delight in claiming that our apparent choices are really no more than a complex series of chemical reactions in the brain so that we may as well be marionettes. But holding, as they do, to this ridiculous belief, one can see why they are flummoxed by the deliberate swimming of jellyfish, *who have no brains at all.*

In 2020, when the various covid travel restrictions and outright bans emptied Menorca's calas of their tourists, a strange thing happened: *the jellyfish disappeared.* This was unusual, as when we were all put under house arrest to protect ourselves from the virus, the deserted towns and waterways were reinhabited by goats and dolphins and other animals. And yet Menorca's jellyfish did the exact opposite and vanished along with the tourists. Why? Could it be that, despite not having a brain, jellyfish are assembling to drive us from the sea *on purpose*? Consider a further curious fact. The world's coastline is disfigured by enormous power stations, which suck in cooling water and spew it out again hot and often irradiated. Jellyfish have a distinct *penchant* for shutting these power stations down by blocking their pipes. Might this be *deliberate*? Are jellyfish protecting the sea from *us*?

My swim beneath the cliffs was not my only encounter with Menorca's jellyfish. Another swimhiking route is thwarted when a school of jellyfish place themselves right in the middle of it. A red flag is flying over the cala when I arrive (they have green, yellow and red warning flags depending on the number of jellyfish in the water) and my fellow holidaymakers are sat disconsolately on the rocks. But it is only a matter of yards to swim from one side to the other. Surely I might risk it? I peer down into the water. There they are again, *Pelagia Noctiluca*, lots of them. I go round the edge.

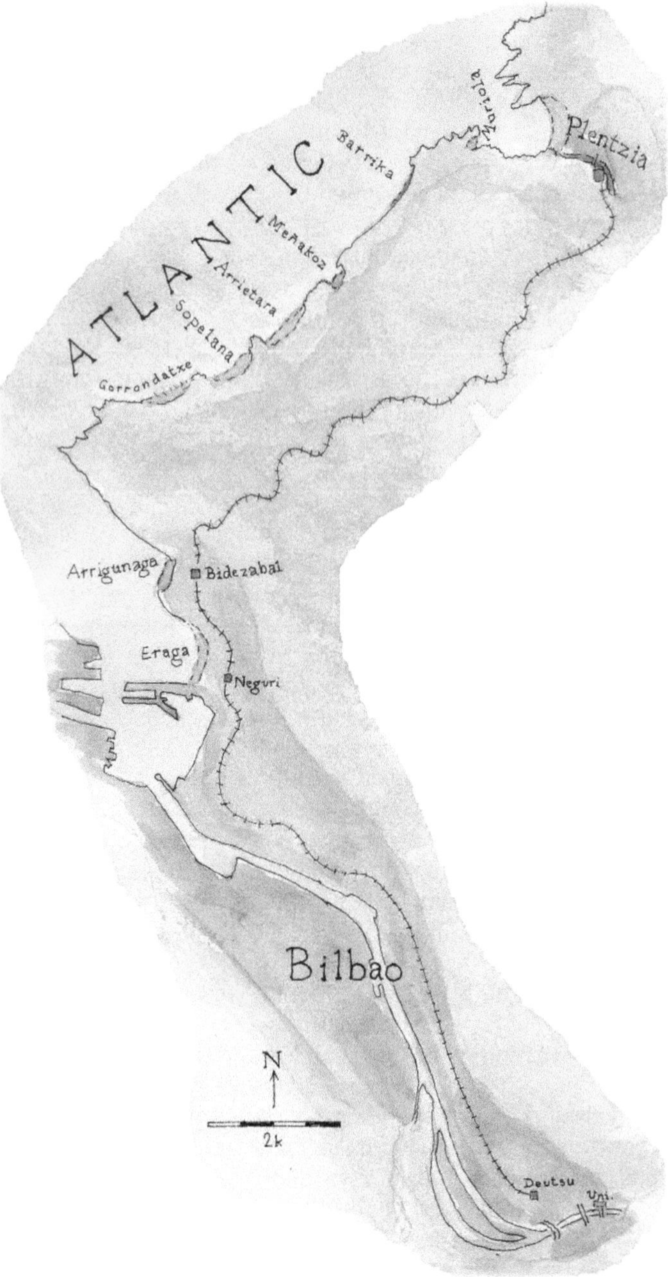

ATLANTIC

Barrika

Meñakoz

Arrietara

Sopelana

Gorrondatxe

Gorliz

Plentzia

Arrigunaga   ▪ Bidezabal

Eraga

▪ Neguri

Bilbao

N

2 k

Deutsu

Uni.

43. Bilbao

I did not have high expectations of Bilbao, which I associated with heavy industry and Basque terrorism. But neither of these things were a problem. Its terrorists had already announced that they would stop murdering people back in 2011 and, as things turned out, I never did visit the industrial area. From what I *did* see, Bilbao is one of the finest cities in Europe. Its modern centre is architecturally stunning. It has a charming old quarter, an excellent art museum, green hills all around, and it is full of exceptionally beautiful women. It is also an easy train or metro ride to the nearest beach Eraga, for a shoreline swimhike, and from the next beach at Arrigunaga, you can walk and swim—and doubtless swimhike—all the way along the coast at a series of ever more delightful beaches until you reach the outskirts of Plentzia. Here a developer seems to have tried to stop up the path, although you can get through. Then, once you are in the town, you are warned not to swim in the river, under penalty of a large fine. You can though, swimhike across the bay. Then you can catch another train back.

Although swimhiking in the river at Plentzia may be financially risky, back in Bilbao there are no such signs around the Ria de Bilbao, or at least I did not notice any when scouting it out. It is a sensible idea, when stepping into a large river, to know in advance exactly how you will be getting out again. So, the night before the planned swimhike, I carefully reconnoitred both the entry and exit points. At Deusto University there is a slope into the water. Good—that will make for an easy way in. And just below the Euskalsduna Bridge there is a floating canoe dock where three boys are having great fun jumping into the water, climbing out on a ladder, and jumping in again. Great—an ideal way out!

The next morning, everything goes smoothly. The tidal river is flowing nicely downstream, the water feels pleasant and there are no boats. I swim out into the middle of the river and enjoy the view of the city as it slips by. How much better this is than to be a mere

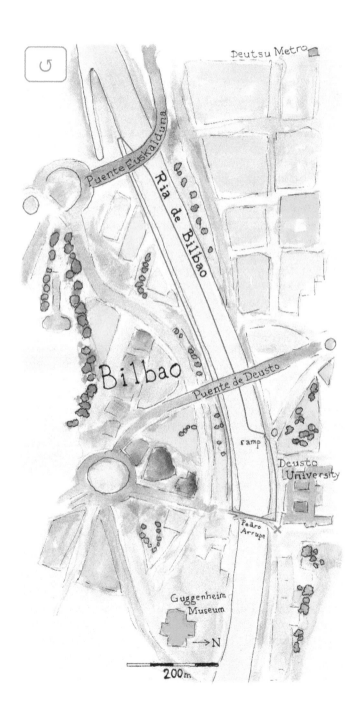

jogger on the bank! I am being gently carried in the direction I want to go and barely need to swim. Now I am under the Euskalduna Bridge, and there is the floating dock with its ladder at the far end. Its ladder. ... Ladder. ... Where *is* the ladder?

It is not there.

Someone has obviously removed the ladder and I am shocked and indignant. I cannot, however, afford to indulge these feelings for long, as the current is continuing to push me downstream and I must decide whether to try and get out at the dock, or to float on down into Bilbao's industrial sector and take my chances there.

I try and get out. This is not easy; there is at least an eighteen-inch gap between the surface of the river and the dockside, there is nothing to stand on in the deep water, and nor is there anything to rest against, as the gap beneath the floating dock means there is no surface on which to steady oneself. But there *is* a boat tie on the dock, which I grab, and then start to heave myself out. It is harder than I thought, and my swimsac feels unusually heavy (later I find that the inner has leaked). I fall back into the water. I try again. And this time, with grim determination, I lever and scrape myself onto the dock. Victory! My elbows are bruised and my knees are bloody. Impressively bloody, I decide. Very tough! Even more victorious! And I jog back along the riverbank feeling proud of them. Getting out of the river at Bilbao is—until I visit Monaco—my hardest ever water egress.

Portugal

Madeira

There are some beaches on Madeira, but mostly there is a rocky shoreline with few sheltered spots to protect against the Atlantic. Here the sea can be difficult to access, as I discovered when I was felled by a wave and knocked about a bit. Madeira's beautiful countryside has a different access problem: it is full of private property, fences and dogs. However, cutting though them all are the levadas, water conduits with public paths by their sides that are very handy for hiking and, of course, swimhiking (though not actually *in* the conduits).

It is also possible to swim around Lido Island. The loop is straightforward; there is no current when I circle the rock. However,

1. ↻ **Levada dos Piornais**

2. ↻ Ilheu do Lido

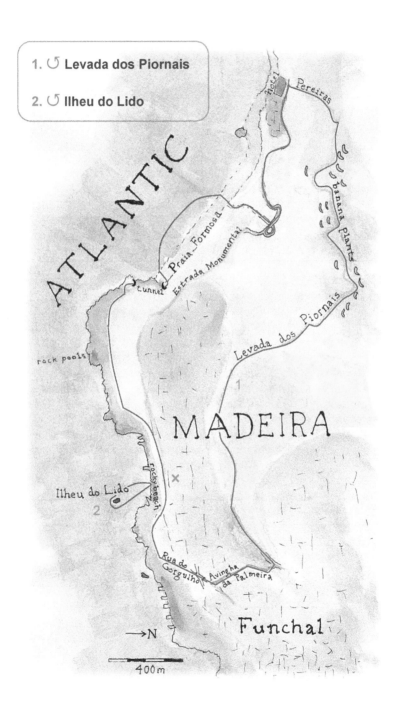

I do have the distinct and uncomfortable feeling that there are *fish* underneath me.

"So what if there are fish? Fish are just fish." I tell myself.

"I know," I reply. "But these ones are different. These are *fish*."

Later that day we visited Funchal Market. Lying on beds of ice were rows of Black scabbardfish, hundreds of them. They were three foot long with ferocious teeth. No other fish were on sale: it seems that these are the only fish to be caught around Madeira. I suppose they eat all the others. And yet, with iron self control, these fish *never eat us tourists*. Rather, it is *we* who eat them, in restaurants that tempt us in with a tame parrot at the entrance.

A lizard we encountered on the island was less restrained than the admirable scabbardfish. Nicholas had discovered that by placing his hand on the ground, curious small lizards would edge up to explore it, and the braver ones would crawl on to it. After watching this for a bit, another somewhat larger lizard came up and bit Nicholas' finger. This was, perhaps, only to be expected as this particular lizard was evidently a bully; we had already seen it fighting and chasing the others. Still, it showed that bully-lizard, and by extension all the other the lizards, knew that the hand was not some inanimate object, but that of a living being—and obviously one that, by its size, could do them harm. The other lizards must also have known that while most creatures might have a reasonable live-and-let live approach to life, there were some, like bully-lizard, who did not. Why then—given that it served no useful purpose whatsoever—did lizards take the risk of crawling around on Nicholas' hand? I think they did it partly because of the urge to explore, experience and enjoy the world around them, and partly because it made life a bit more exciting for them. And this, I think, is rather like swimhiking.

Epilogue

When I started to prepare this book, it was with a sense of nostalgia for Europe before Brexit, when we were still part of an organisation that, for all of its flaws, seemed to have at least partially realised the goals of the visionary pontiffs in becoming a peaceful, hospitable place that bridged cultural gaps. Two years later, I find myself feeling nostalgic for the brief period in early 2020 *after* we had left the EU but *before* covid. The petty ignominies devised for British travellers back then—the queues, the otiose paperwork, the smirking border guards confiscating sandwiches—all these now seem as nothing.

One of the things I love most about swimhiking in Europe is the sight of all the beautiful and colourful fish in the Mediterranean. British fish, by contrast, are hard to spot and comparatively dull. For the sight of these beautiful fish, I might even submit to the extra covid vaccinations, without which large parts of the Mediterranean are now closed to me. But I am reluctant. The overreaction to covid has not been confined to Europe. All over the world, the warm community spirit of the early pandemic seems to have been supplanted by a kind of mania. Surely, this can only be temporary; there are already welcome signs of a return to common sense and perhaps all the prohibitions and rules will soon fade away like a bad dream; I should hold my nerve. But if the history of Europe teaches us anything, it is that common sense can be a rare commodity and that we actually seem to quite like indulging in various forms of collective madness. What if there is only a further downward spiral?

And now we have the sudden, awful madness of Russia's invasion of Ukraine.

Whatever next?

But to return to my personal dilemma. If I need X-number of vaccines to travel to the Med, I think to myself, why not just give in, and accept that, henceforward, this is just a part of the price that I will have to pay? It may not be just but, as Thucydides puts it, the powerful take what they can and the weak accept what they must. And after all, I never bother to wear beach shoes when I walk down the sand to go swimming in the sea off Pembrokeshire, and risk treading on a weever fish without a second thought. Well then, isn't being jabbed with a vaccine on the way to a swim in the Mediterranean more or less the same as being jabbed by a weever fish in Pembrokeshire, only less painful? But then, I think, I would hardly go treading on a weever fish *deliberately*. And all the while, vaguely nagging at my conscience, is the idea that trading jabs for foreign holidays betrays all those people who have lost their livelihoods for trying to defend our right to bodily integrity.

But who cares about my predicament? It doesn't really matter whether I get back into the warm waters of the Mediterranean or not; I have had my time there. It is *you* who I very much hope will be able to go and enjoy a wonderful time swimhiking there, and indeed everywhere in Europe and Britain too.

Take care! Whenever there is reason for doubt, check-out your exit point *before* you enter the water! Try not to tread on a weever fish, and try to not tread on a sea urchin either. However, if you *do* tread on a sea urchin, you now know what to do: go to a pharmacy and ask for Black Pasta.

Peter Hayes
March 2022

187

Lightning Source UK Ltd.
Milton Keynes UK
UKHW021433300322
400816UK00006B/85